MESSAGES
TO THE
FUTURE

MESSAGES
TO THE
FUTURE

Director of Education, LB Bromley
Ken Davis

Millennium Arts Project Directors
Pamela Smyth and Jay Mathews

DTP Design
Ray Bryant

Editors
Gillian Cooling
Lauren Robertson

Design
Ray Mathews
Floyd Sayers
Anthony Cutting

Art Director
Chez Picthall

Editorial Director
Christiane Gunzi

Project Consultants
Jan Sage and Christopher Town

Project Administrator
Pauline Lupton-Dewell

Cover Illustrations
Renate Keeping & Pupils

First published in Great Britain in 2000
by Picthall & Gunzi Limited,
21 Widmore Road,
Bromley, Kent BR1 1RW

Cover reproduction by Digicol, Bromley, Kent
Printed and bound in Italy, by LEGOPRINT

ISBN 0-9537785-0-9

CONTENTS

FOREWORD

WELCOME...
...TO BROMLEY'S MILLENNIUM ANTHOLOGY

To mark the Millennium, children and young people in schools across Bromley have written and illustrated their hopes, promises and thoughts for the future.

These have been collected in a stunning array of school anthologies which will be displayed in exhibitions in Bromley and in the Millennium Dome.

The anthology you are reading now collects together just a small sample of all this work. Each school has chosen the pieces to go on their own page. Enjoy your reading.

Pamela Smyth
Co-director, Millennium Arts Project
General Adviser, Standards & Effectiveness Services,
London Borough of Bromley

I congratulate
Members of
The Forum for the Arts in Bromley for Learning in Education
on their whole hearted support of
Bromley's Millennium Festival
and wish them every success with their event(s).

signed Sue Polydorou

The Worshipful the Mayor of Bromley
Councillor Sue Polydorou, JP

TO YOU ALL

I am delighted to present this anthology of children's work. It represents a tremendous effort by everyone involved. I am sure you will enjoy reading the wide-ranging and thought-provoking contributions made by so many of our children and young people – the citizens of our future.

The anthology represents the culmination of lots of thoughtful and concerned responses to what the future might hold at this turning point in history. Children and young people have been involved in projects to celebrate the National Year of Reading, which is part of The National Literacy Strategy. It will be inspiring for all these young writers to see their work professionally published.

Schools are already involved in preparing many other wonderful projects for this Millennium Year. I look forward to enjoying them with you.

My thanks to everyone involved.

Ken Davis
Director of Education,
London Borough of Bromley

DEAR CITIZENS OF THE FUTURE

This wonderful anthology is enduring proof that, when people work together with a shared vision to create something worthwhile – great things can happen!

In 1999, the young people of Bromley and their teachers shared such a vision, and this book is the result.

Always believe that what you do is important!

Good luck in the future.

Jay Mathews
Co-director, Millennium Arts Project
Associate Consultant, Standards & Effectiveness Services,
London Borough of Bromley

DEAR READERS

I am pleased to add my message of support to this exciting anthology. I recognise all the hard work and creativity that has made it possible. What a pleasure it is to read all these stories, hopes and wishes, prayers, poems and promises for the future from the children and young people of our borough.

My congratulations and good wishes to all concerned.

Ernie Dyer
Chair of the Education Committee,
London Borough of Bromley

MY WISH FOR THE MILLENIUM

I hope people will not find the need
   for cruelty prejudice and greed.
Enjoy each other, play their parts in music,
   drama and the arts.
Sing their song, discard the knife
   and . . . Have a good life!

Renate Keeping
Artist

A MESSAGE TO THE FUTURE

It has been a great pleasure for us to be involved in producing this special anthology, and this book could not have happened without the hundreds of school children who contributed their stories, poems, messages, wishes, prayers and pictures in celebration of the new Millennium. Read what they have to say – they are an inspiration to us all!

Christiane Gunzi & Chez Picthall
Picthall & Gunzi Ltd

A FABLE PROMISE

This innovative anthology marks a milestone in the work of the Forum for the Arts in Bromley for Learning in Education. FABLE has been helping to develop the arts in education in Bromley since 1995. It will continue to support schools and arts organisations in ensuring that creativity in all its forms inspires and motivates children's learning into the new Millennium.

The FABLE Steering Group
Yvette Bellis, Andy Booth, Toni Cox, Mike Day, Kevin Dyke,
Gill Finch and Pamela Smyth

MY HOPES FOR THE FUTURE

"Every child and student should have an experience of school that is memorable; memorable because they each laughed a lot, learned a lot and had a lasting experience, which will help them to be flexible, adaptable, confident and self-disciplined in a fast-changing world, yet, at the same time, to be sensitive to the needs of others."

The School Curriculum – *A Framework of Principles*

"The more technological our world becomes,
the more poems, songs and stories
our children need."

Chris Green
Assistant Director of Education,
Standards & Effectiveness Services,
London Borough of Bromley

Dear Future Reader Of
The 31st Century

Hi, my name is Steven and I am writing to someone in the hope that they may read this. It is strange to think that when somebody reads this they will be living in a whole new world. I am looking forward to the future, I bet you are frequently landing on the Moon, flying around in spinners and living on Mars. It is 1999, we are nearing the Millennium, but none of these things is evenly remotely likely at the moment.

This year has been full of wars, bombs, fights and deaths. It is not a happy world that we live in, but I hope you are not still arguing and fighting. We are happy most of the time and for entertainment I go to the cinema, the arcade or to the local snooker club. Not very exciting, as I am sure you have massive casinos and halls of billiard tables.

Our summers are very hot now, perhaps too hot for some people and the way global warming is going, you must be living in a tropical paradise.

Well, the Millennium is just over seven months away now and as many people are excited and looking forward to it, some people are frightened about what might happen. There is the big possibility of the Millennium Bug arriving, causing thousands of old computers, hospital equipment and even planes to crash. This could be absolutely devastating, putting companies out of business and killing many innocent people. Fewer people think that the world will end, with volcanoes, earthquakes and the arrival of Jesus. Nobody knows really what is going to happen, we all just have to hope for the best.

I seriously hope that you are all living in peace and can solve your problems without fighting, and I hope that there is no more poverty or illness. It is so sad to think that we start wars over such stupid things, and millions of people are poor and living on the streets. My ambition in life is to basically travel all around the world. I want to see the sights, enjoy myself and hopefully help some people in any way I can. When someone has read this, all I ask for from them is to think of me and remember me. I wish you all the best and good luck for the future.

Regards,

Steven, writing from the near 21st century

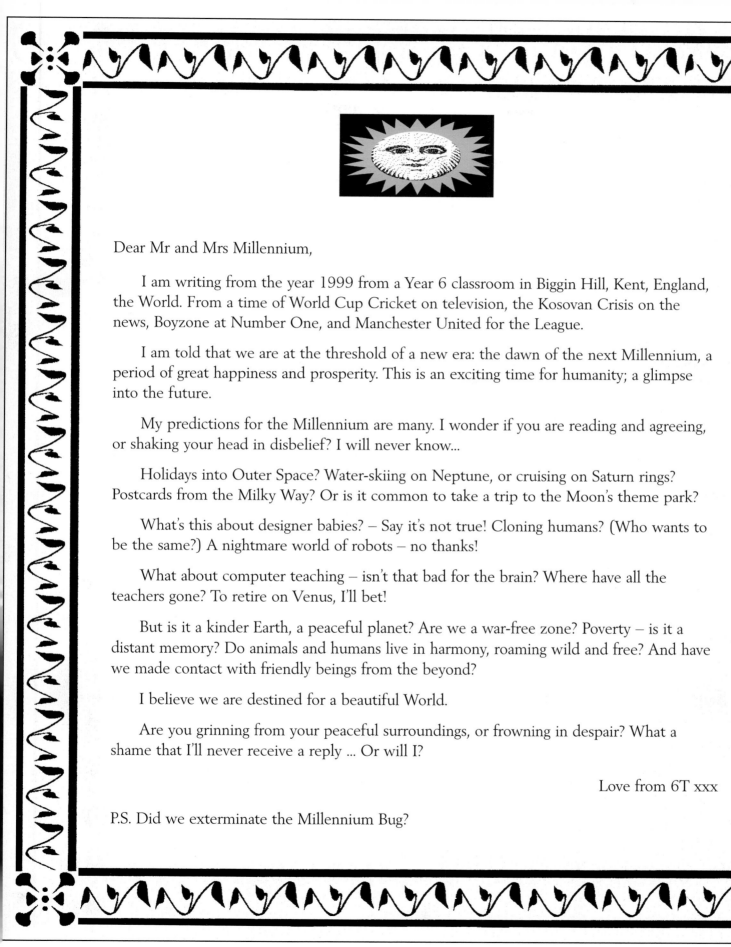

Dear Mr and Mrs Millennium,

I am writing from the year 1999 from a Year 6 classroom in Biggin Hill, Kent, England, the World. From a time of World Cup Cricket on television, the Kosovan Crisis on the news, Boyzone at Number One, and Manchester United for the League.

I am told that we are at the threshold of a new era: the dawn of the next Millennium, a period of great happiness and prosperity. This is an exciting time for humanity; a glimpse into the future.

My predictions for the Millennium are many. I wonder if you are reading and agreeing, or shaking your head in disbelief? I will never know...

Holidays into Outer Space? Water-skiing on Neptune, or cruising on Saturn rings? Postcards from the Milky Way? Or is it common to take a trip to the Moon's theme park?

What's this about designer babies? – Say it's not true! Cloning humans? (Who wants to be the same?) A nightmare world of robots – no thanks!

What about computer teaching – isn't that bad for the brain? Where have all the teachers gone? To retire on Venus, I'll bet!

But is it a kinder Earth, a peaceful planet? Are we a war-free zone? Poverty – is it a distant memory? Do animals and humans live in harmony, roaming wild and free? And have we made contact with friendly beings from the beyond?

I believe we are destined for a beautiful World.

Are you grinning from your peaceful surroundings, or frowning in despair? What a shame that I'll never receive a reply ... Or will I?

Love from 6T xxx

P.S. Did we exterminate the Millennium Bug?

ALEXANDRA INFANT SCHOOL

*I hope I still know my best friend when I'm older.
I hope me and my friend are the
best of friends.*

SOPHIE GUIDERA, AGED 7

*I am being a friend to someone who is sad.
I am holding their hand.*

WILLIAM JUDGE, AGED 5

We make each other happy.

RECEPTION CLASS, AGED 5

We help each other when we are hurt.

RECEPTION CLASS, AGED 5

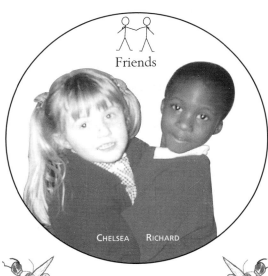

Friends

CHELSEA   RICHARD

DREW TOWNLEY, AGED 6

Friends   **are**   **good.**

HÉLOÏSE PELIGRY, AGED 6

Make   the   world

a   happy place.

*Stop cutting down the trees because us animals
need them. If you don't, I will screech in your ear.*

LUCY GARWOOD, AGED 6

Friends are good because they play with you.

MARTHA WAISWA, AGED 7

*I hope everyone lives in harmony in the future.
I hope everyone likes each other.*

STEPHEN BRIDGER, AGED 7

Alexandra Junior School

Who's That?

Who's that?
Who's that lurking in the bushes?
It is us, the animal protectors,
    and we are watching you,
    shooting the wild animals.

Who's that?
Who's that whirling and twirling in the purple sky?
It is us, the sky fairies,
    and we are watching you,
    polluting the charming air.

Who's that?
Who's that bouncing up and down on the cliffs?
It is us, the sea elves,
    and we are watching you,
    poison our lovely glittery sea home.

Who's that?
Who's that blowing bubbles in the light blue sea?
It is us, the dolphin kings and queens for the future,
    and we are watching you,
    killing the lovely colourful fishes.

SHERYL WILLIS, AGED 9

Who's There?

Who's there?
Who's there hiding behind the sand and
    seaweed slithering through the rocks?
It's us, the Cotjotters, and we are watching you,
    filling our sea with rubbish and poison.

Who's there?
Who's there lurking behind the rocks?
It's us, the Sharkins and the Divers,
    and we are watching you,
Killing the sharks just for their fins and
    sending them to extinction.

Who's there?
Who's there camouflaged in the bushes
    squelching through the mud?
It's us, the Warins and the Armans,
    and we are watching you,
Killing each other with guns and knives
    teaming up in armies and fighting in wars.

Who's there?
Who's there hiding behind the stars, darting past galaxies?
It's us, the Worldoes and the Earthons,
    and we are watching you,
The guardians of the world protecting our planet
    and the living things.

JACK BOWYER AND HARRY ROCHESTER, AGED 9

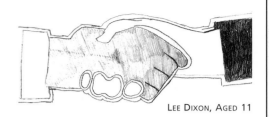

LEE DIXON, AGED 11

In The Future ...

I would like to see:
The beautiful colourful
    butterflies flying,
The faintness of the stars,
The softness of the air,
The freshness of the grass.

LEANNE WEBB AND EMEL MUSLU, AGED 9

In The Future ...

I don't want to see:
Animals destroyed,
Polluted streams,
Wastelands.
I would like to see:
The splashing of silver waterfalls,
Beautiful bluebells spreading,
Golden rivers and lakes,
The sound of the sea.

JOSEPH ANDERSON, AGED 9

JAKE FAN, AGED 8

Millennium

Music plays down the streets of London
I stand in the middle of a frantic crowd
Laughter travels like fire spreading across an open field
Little sparks of excitement turn into giant explosions
Even I start to enjoy the celebration
Now I look at people with bright smiles on their faces
New people join the joyful crowd
I see families trying to escape from the streets
Until they are trapped in the middle of the excitement
Must they join the celebration or should they?

JAMES BUCKLE, AGED 10

ANERLEY PRIMARY SCHOOL

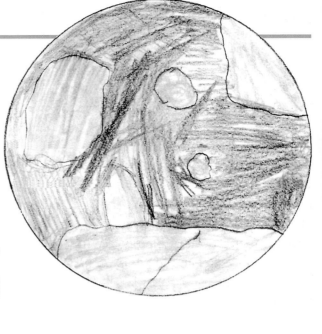

WISH FOR THE FUTURE

*I hope that peace will spread around the world
and people will stop bombing other countries.
I wish that the world be a safer place.
It would be nice if people were given a second chance in life.*

ROBYN HANNON, AGED 9

PARADISE THE FUTURE?

Happiness bringer,

Evil killer,

Peace keeper,

Animal lover,

Weapon destroyer,

Bad killer,

Soul taker,

Love bringer,

Happiness maker,

Flower lover,

Nice land maker,

Love bringer,

Relationship maker,

Family helper,

Tree keeper.

PARADISE!

SHARLEEN KWARTENG AND
LERESHA THOMPSON, AGED 11

KELLY NOSHIE, AGED 9

RICHARD MONK, AGED 5

MARCUS McFOY, AGED 7

ROCHELLE GREENIDGE, AGED 5

MILLENNIUM MESSAGE

Please make people and animals free from hunters and soldiers. The world should be peaceful and caring with kindness for others. People who are in hospital should get more treatment, and people in wheelchairs should have a slope or lift to go up and down in the supermarkets. Be respectful to people, but don't speak to strangers.

CAROLINE PRIDEAUX, AGED 8

ALEX ELSE, AGED 8

ROSEANNE CUMMINGS, AGED 7

I wish that everyone could have a mum and dad.

OMAR SILAS II, AGED 7

Balgowan Primary School

In The Future

When you come out of the super-market there will be a big hissing noise. Some flaps will open from the ceiling and millions of robots will come out of the holes. They are not just normal robots, they are very clever robots. They are helpful as well. When they run out of energy, a wire comes out of their body and it holds a battery in it and it puts the battery in the robot's head.

The robots have brushes on their feet so when they walk it makes the floor shine. They have cloths on their hands so when they touch anything it gets really clean. The robots also have hoovers on their heads so when they are standing still the hoover reaches right up to the ceiling and makes the ceiling really clean. That is how you clean a supermarket.

ANDREW REEVES, AGED 7

Wishes For The Millennium

I wish the Moon could speak to people when they were naughty.
FRANCESCA McKIBBON

I wish everyone was kind.
SAM O'DONNELL

I wish that all the houses would have tinsel and little lanterns round them for the Millennium.
HELENA KERNAN

I wish my dad didn't smoke.
CHRISTOPHER DUDLEY

I wish everyone had a rabbit to cuddle.
MEGAN TURNER

I wish that all the people in the town would love everybody.
JAMES PHILLIPS

I wish my cat can talk.
AMY HOUGHAM

I wish there was money to buy food for everybody.
JONATHAN LEE-AKIN

I wish for a doctor to make people better.
ISOBEL STEPHENSON

I wish everyone was happy.
DANIEL MORRIS

I wish we had the biggest library in the world.
KATIE STANNARD

RECEPTION CLASS, AGED 4–5

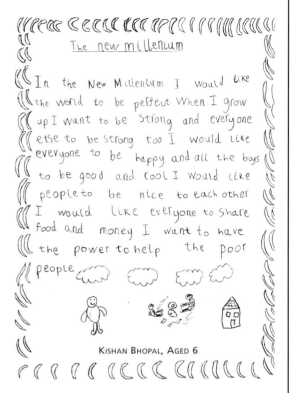

The new millenium

In the New Millenium I would like the world to be perfect. When I grow up I want to be strong and everyone else to be strong too. I would like everyone to be happy and all the boys to be good and cool. I would like people to be nice to each other I would like everyone to share food and money. I want to have the power to help the poor people.

KISHAN BHOPAL, AGED 6

Ozone Man !

One day Ozone Man left his home in Luxembourg and flew around the world doing his job of mending the Ozone layer. (Which he does every day at 6:00am) "Nobody cares what I'm doing everyone takes it for granted."
"I'm fed up with getting up at 6:00am every morning and mending the ozone layer" "People aren't helping by cutting down trees and all the pollution from cars, I'm not going to mend the ozone layer for a few years and see how they cope," Said Ozone Man furiously. Five years later all the trees had been cut down, skin cancer had increased by 75%, polar ice caps had melted, a vast amount of land throughout the world had flooded, which meant more people caught diseases from the sewers. Ozone Man saw how it had changed and said to the world, "I will mend the Ozone layer only if the whole world stops cutting the trees down and grows more trees to replace the rain forest, also cuts down on pollution to decrease carbon dioxide and other poisonous gases" The leaders of the world agreed with Ozone Man, and they all promised to help him to save the planet and make the world a better place.

JOEL BENFIELD, AGED 10

Message To The Future

I am not yet born; O hear me
What a wonderful and peaceful world
No wars, no fighting, and no arguing
A very good start to the new Millennium

I am not yet born; O look at me
The new technological development
Robot cleaners, space travel agencies
all around the cities
One day, worldwide travel will definitely
be my choice

We are not yet born; O feel ourselves
We are so happy
Freedom and wisdom belong to us forever
Please come and join us

ANNE XU, AGED 15

The Millispeed

The millispeed can fly, hover, drive normally or fly like a rocket. It is powered
by pure gel which does not pollute the
air or sky or even water.
It is perfectly safe.

NICOLE CONOLLY, AGED 10

Hey diddle diddle
The mouse and computer
The rocket zoomed over
the Moon
The Millennium Bug laughed
To see such fun
And the screen ran away with
the printer

GEORGINA, JENI, CHRISTIE,
JESSICA, ALEXANDRA, ALICE
AND GILLY, AGED 8–9

Wish For The Future

We wish for the future
A future with no bombs
No wars
No fighting
No killing

We wish for the future
A future with lots of kindness
Time for each other
Time to stop and look
Time to smile

We wish for the future
A future with a sunny sky
With butterflies which talk
With flowers that walk
Where people love animals
Not kill them

We wish for the future
A future with a clean world
Where we put our cars away
Locking up the exhaust
Riding our bicycles
Jumping on the bus

We wish for the future
A future where we are safe
Not frightened
Where we are well
Not choked to death
Where we can laugh

YEAR 1, AGED 5–6

The Millennium Dome Is Falling Down, Falling Down, Falling Down!

Last night, at about 8 o'clock there was a
dreadful crash. Somebody noticed that the
Millennium Dome was falling down.
It made such a loud noise that the whole of
London heard it. We are now concentrating
on cleaning up the great mess that was left
behind. All the materials will be recycled. The
money that was spent on the Dome
was 50 million pounds.

FELICITY CHRISTIAANS, AGED 11

History

What would make History?
Is it such a mystery?
Men having babies,
An injection for rabies,
Solar cars,
Life on Mars,
Robots thinking,
Whilst land is sinking,
Is it such a mystery?

NICOLA MORLEY, AGED 14

The warm, white soft sand,
As it filters through my hand,
Buries memories.

ELEANOR STOKES, AGED 13

It's time to make a diff-erence Time to change this world Put all that's bad be-hind us Make a bright new fu-ture Make a bright new fu-ture Put all that's bad be-hind us Make a bright new fu-ture Put all that's bad be-hind us

KATIE COX, AGED 15

bright new fu-t ure It's time to make a diff-erence Time to change this world Put

ALEX

Paris

Zoe

Pablo

LUke

Shannon.

Rachel.

Shavaun

Anthony.

Callum

Chloe

Cole

Ewan

George

OUR SCHOOL SONG

We are the School, the children of the world;

we hold tomorrow in our hands.

We are the school, the children

of a bright new start; the

future's here in our new school.

Teach us well, teach us how to care;

teach us love, love that we may share.

For the walls of our school tell a tale of the

children past. We are the School!

We make friends With each other it's fun with a friend.

SHAVAUN MacARTHUR, AGED 5

In our new school we play together.

ALEX HOLMES, AGED 5

Stephen

Kotel

Louis

Mark

In our new school we Like doing our work.

JAMES STEAD, AGED 5

RECEPTION CLASS

OUR SCHOOL SPORTS DAY

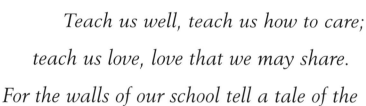

ANTHONY McCARTHY, AGED 5

Matth ew

Natalie

Grace

Jake

James e

James

James S.

Paisley

Oliver

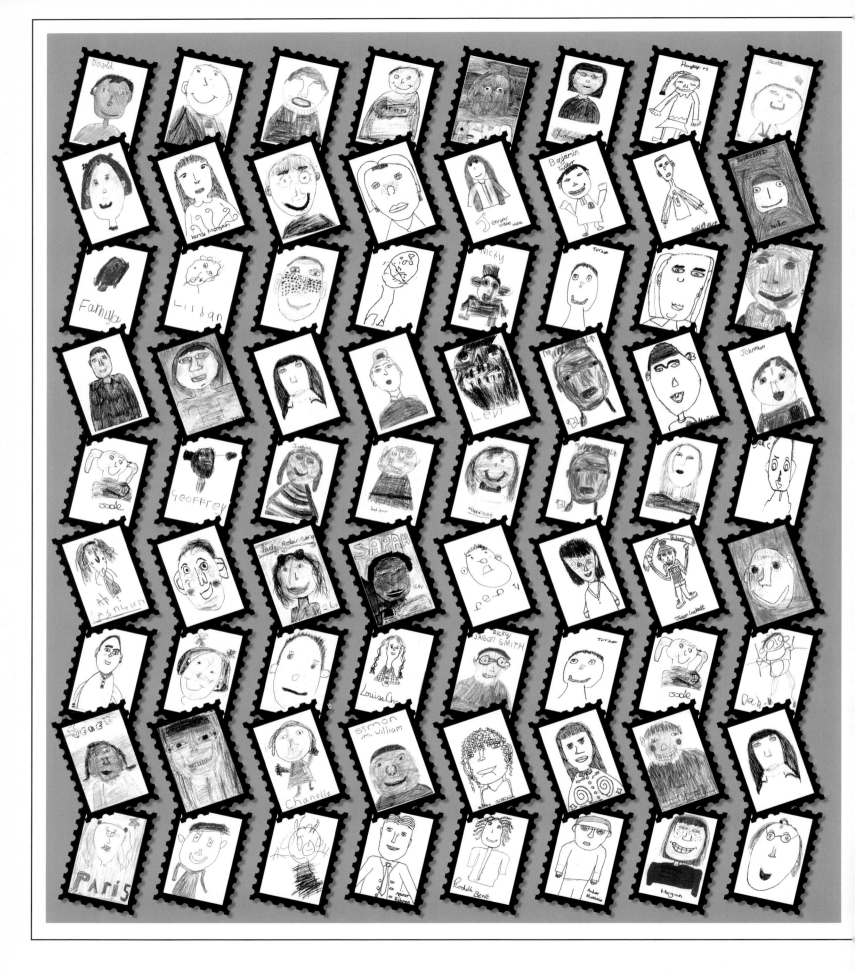

Biggin Hill Infant School

Me And My Biscuits

One day after school my mum said I had to have one biscuit but I had two biscuits. Then I had ... **NONE** because Mum took them and Mum had them.

Moral: Be grateful for what you have.

ANTHONY PAYNE, AGED 7

A car that does not need petrol and drives itself.

The Rat And The Cat

The rat went to the park.
The cat followed the rat.

Moral: Don't follow people when they don't want you to.

BECKY PURNELL, AGED 6

A Rainforest Spreading

ROBERT BLACKBURN, AGED 7

Hickory Dickory Doo

Hickory Dickory Doo,
The duck jumped into the shoe,
The clock struck two,
The duck fell through,
Hickory Dickory Doo.

CLASS YD (RECEPTION), AGED 4

A bed that bounces you out of bed when it is time to get out of bed.

LUKAS CHOPPEN, AGED 7

I hope the world is going to be a clean world.

GEMMA JORDANA, AGED 7

I hope that everyone will look after the world.

JOSEPH WALSHE, AGED 7

I hope the world is still a happy place.

B-J TARBIE, AGED 6

The Mouse And His Friend

ONCE UPON A TIME there were two mice and they were the best of friends. But there was a mouse trap and if any mouse got stuck in it they would die. But there was a mouse who did not believe that this was a real mouse trap, so one day he took his best friend and said, "Let's go and see that thing." "No, it's a mouse trap!" "Oh, don't be a baby," he said. "That is just a picture." But his friend would not go, so he dragged her along to the mouse trap and she got stuck in it and, of course, she died.

Moral: Look at it before you do it.

LAUREN RAWLINS, AGED 6

The Mouse And A Lion

The mouse went to a field.
The mouse saw the lion.
The lion saw the mouse.
The lion ate up the mouse,
every little bit.

Moral: You shouldn't eat anybody up.

TIMOTHY THOMPSON, AGED 6

Me I wrote a message to Lizzy

Lizzy sent an E-mail to Jack

TODAY ...

Today we have electricity
How would a day go past
without electricity?
We wouldn't have any phones,
or appliances.

Today we have countryside.
How would a day go past
without countryside?
We wouldn't have trees to
help us breathe.

Today we have people.
How would a day go past
without people?
We would have peace.

LOUISE PERRY, AGED 11

MOVING FUTURE HAIKU

Time is everything
2000 time, coming fast
Moving change ahead.

YEAR 4, AGED 9

MESSAGE IN A HAIKU

The postman comes with
a special message for me.
What is the message?

"Dear Jim, greetings from
a future Millennium!
Can't wait to see you."

DOUGLAS NORTON AND LIAM TYRRELL, AGED 10

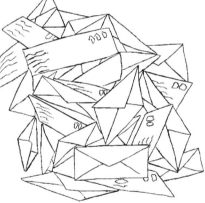

LUKE MANTOURA, AGED 11

Do the trees sway?
Do children still play?
Are you still very hot?
Or is the Earth just not?
Do you fly through space,
at an unnerving pace?
Are the oceans rising?
Is the land demising?
Are you underwater?
Still building with bricks
and mortar?
Is there someone reading?
Or are you all pleading
to stay alive on Earth?

ARWEN LANE, AGED 11

IMAGINE

Imagine a world without any trees,
Imagine a world without any bees,
Imagine a world without any flowers,
Imagine a world that was dark for hours.

No animals, no people to be seen,
No you nor me, no King nor Queen,
All gone to heaven because we didn't know
How to treat the Earth below.
All because we didn't listen in school,
Because we didn't obey some simple rules.

HANNAH COOL, AGED 8

MOONLIGHT SPACE HAIKU

Stars twinkle in space
Exploring the Universe
Mankind lay asleep

YEAR 4, AGED 9

Animals, animals, wonderful pets,
Nobody should catch them in nets.
Imagine a world with no animals near,
Maybe it seems a little bit queer.
All the species must survive centuries more.
Little of them have a life,
So don't kill them with a knife.

DANIEL CONANT, AGED 8

Alice sent a telegram to Alice

Amy sent a message in a bottle to Alice

LEE HARDING, AGED 10

put a postcard in the postbox

Sent a fax to Lee Lee

Jack sent a birthday card to Mr Pullen Mr Pullen

BLENHEIM INFANT SCHOOL

MY MILLENNIUM SCHOOL

My classroom furniture I have chairs and tables. I have computers and TV. My glass is orange and orange curtains are there. The children are being kind to other people.

MOLLY REEVE, AGED 6

A brush that cleans on its own. A safe to keep things in. The children will be on the computer.

JAMES PASK, AGED 5

Yes the school will be different because I won't be there. I will be a dad.

BEN BARNETT, AGED 5

MY MILLENNIUM UNIFORM

I would like to be Action man. I would like to be Batman.

SCOTT CARD, AGED 5

MY HOPES FOR THE MILLENNIUM

I hope that money grows on trees and flowers, so everybody can be rich, kind, and helpful. I hope that wars stop so people can be safe and travel around the world to explore. I hope the grass is green all the time because it is pretty, and there should be enough water and clothes for poor countries because it is sad when they don't have enough. I want there to be a swimming pool in my house and every house, and when God looks down on the Earth he will see no rubbish.

LYNNE OLIVER, AGED 7

WHEN I GROW UP

I hope when I grow up I'll be a policeman, because I want to help people in robberies.

LEIGH HAWKES, AGED 7

MY YEAR 2000 PLAYGROUND

My millennium playground I want to have a slide.

SAM BAINES, AGED 6

I would like a football pitch. I would like a toy motorbike.

DANIEL NOEL-DAVIES, AGED 6

I want to have a swimming pool to splash in. I would like a big tall tall slide. I would like it to be a really good playground. I would like a bouncy castle.

RACHEL BEALING, AGED 6

CIRCUIT BOARD CITY

IT WAS MY DAD'S BIRTHDAY. He was going to have a surprise party. I had bought him a green shirt, to match his new tie. I looked around the house for a place to hide his present and thought of a gap behind the bookcase.

As I went behind the bookcase, I fell back into a strange place. It was like a junk yard, with lots of strange black houses. There were no trees or any green plants. A massive electrical object stood at the edge of the city. There were lots of holes around it, where there had been explosions!

"Where am I?"
"You are in Circuit Board City," replied a strange voice.
"What!" I gasped.
"Make sure you do not come out at night.

Robots, half men and half machinery, will attack you!"

Night came. The robots came as if they knew I was there. They grabbed me. I was so scared as they threw me into a dark room, like a dungeon. There in the darkness was someone else. He told me that I had to find a picture of my house on the computer circuit board behind the guards to get home again. Somehow, I had to sneak up and distract them. I tried so many times but, at last, I managed to touch the picture. I was home again. Imagine my surprise at finding Dad sitting in my chair playing on my PlayStation!

Moral: Always think about whether it is safe to do something. Is it wise to hide things from other people?

JAMES CARTLIDGE, AGED 9

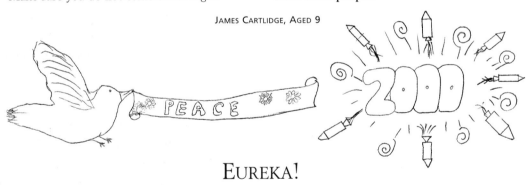

EUREKA!

"EUREKA! I THINK THIS IS IT, I've finally made it!" shouted James, a scientist at the Blenheim Scientific Laboratory.

"I've finally made it," shouted James for the second time.

"What have you made?" the other scientist shouted across curiously.

"I've made a new energy source," replied James excitedly.

"I'm going to show it to the world's top scientists."

"What about the long-term effects, have you studied them?"

"Oh, it will be OK," said James, shoving his

colleague out of the way as he went through the door excitedly.

When he showed it to the top scientists in the country, they were impressed. His energy source was sent all around the world for people to use. James became a multi-millionaire.

All this happened 150 years ago. Now the Earth has only five years left to sustain LIFE!

Moral: Always check things before you play with them, the future may be in danger!

JAMES ASH, AGED 10

DR MICALLEF'S POTION

Dr Micallef was in his laboratory carrying out some experiments. He was a slim man, with grey hair and green eyes. He was a well-known scientist and loved his work.

He walked out of his lab for some fresh air. He looked down and noticed a large, grey shadow covering the ground. He looked up and there above him was a massive spaceship. Why had it come?

A beam of light shone down. Dr Micallef closed his eyes as its force beam lifted him upwards. Inside the spaceship, Dr Micallef came face to face with two aliens. He felt very nervous. Something touched his shoulder. He turned around to see another alien standing there, with a strange-looking object on its head.

The alien took Dr Micallef to a room and said that they had listened to the space waves and heard that Dr Micallef was a great scientist. They needed him to fix their ozone layer. The hole in the ozone layer was killing their people.

Dr Micallef was shown to a laboratory and told to make a special potion. It took him a whole week just to stir up the potion, which he handled with great care. Everyone was really excited. Dr Micallef was very worried in case he dropped the potion. He placed it in a spray can and the next night they opened a hatch in the spaceship and sprayed the potion over the holes in the ozone layer.

The aliens' lives were saved too!

Moral: You may not have a Dr Micallef to look after your ozone layer!

HAYLEY MICALLEF, AGED 10

Bromley High School GDST (Junior Dept)

Stop!

Stop all the greed anywhere, everywhere.
Stop all the wars I declare.
Stop all accidents that are a big mistake.
Stop people stealing, do give – don't take.
Stop people dying in places far away.
Stop all of this I say.

ALIX BLOOMFIELD, AGED 8

Message For The Future

Kosovo is at war. I wish it would stop.
Oh, please stop polluting the air and try to walk more.
So, you're being bullied. Bullying must stop!
On the African plains animals are rare and some extinct.
Vultures are the lucky ones, not like Indian tigers.
Oh, please make more security in schools and don't let
    people have guns.

LOUISE SEDGWICK, AGED 7

CHARLIE WOOLLARD, AGED 5

I hope everyone is kind to other people and they ...

are kind to animals. help people when they're hurt even if they are a different religion.... keep nature going.... and stop other people from ruining it.

EMMA JACOBS, AGED 7

Fumes

First it was there and then it wasn't. Gliding through the city of London, its black fluffy clouds of smoke poisoning everyone in its depths. Its huge arms strangling people as it slips behind all the fast moving cars. Its smell is unbearable, choking people in its path.

If we used cars which ran on batteries it could save many lives. Fumes can cause lung disease and cancer. If we used different forms of transport, like bicycles, which don't run on petrol or coal it would be better. It would give us exercise as well.

CHARLOTTE STAFFORD, AGED 10

My Hope For The Millennium

I hope in the Millennium people care for animals and the people of Kosovo more than they do now. I hope that hunters stop killing animals for their skin. I am glad that some elephants are growing up without any tusks. I hope that more people give money to Kosovo to help the children. They are children too, so why can't they be treated like us? We are very lucky to have parents. Some children, like the children of Kosovo, might not have any.

FRANKIE WILLIAMS, AGED 8

The World Is Lovely

The world is lovely.
It's lovely to read.
It's lovely to learn.
Life is lovely.
God made it all.

MILLIE CROW, AGED 6

Year 2000...

*is full of fireworks and fun.
We'll keep the party going
'til 2001!*

EMILY BARRATT, AGED 9

EMILY HARRIS, AGED 5

Dear Millennium

Are you good, or are you bad?
Are you happy, or are you sad?
Will you help the human race?
Will you give us a friendly face?
Where will we work,
What will we buy?
Will we smile, or will we sigh?
Will future skies be dull or clear?
Will we know, or will we fear?
Are you friend, or are you foe?
Will people's happiness
still show?
Please tell me Millennium,
I need to know.

AMY JONES, AGED 11

BROMLEY HIGH SCHOOL GDST

TIME

Time disappears before we realise that we had it.
It flies out of our hands like a bird.
We must listen to the past, to help us in the future
and, indeed, in the present.
Appreciate time, because before you know it,
it is gone.
Time does not last for us, but it carries on for
others in the future.

CAROLINE HEARN, AGED 14

I'd like the world to be like sunrise,
Fresh yellow, orange, red,
Rising from the mist,
Dew on the grass and flowers uncurling.
I'd like the world to be like a morning garden,
Unspoiled.

OLIVIA FURSE, AGED 12

THE MILLENNIUM BUG

Does it crawl?
Does it bite?
Does it jump?
Is it in sight?

EMMA WRIGHT, AGED 12

Sir or Madam
Any Country
Any Area of Human Habitation

Dear Member of the Human Race,

I am writing this letter to tell you about a great idea. You may have heard of Third World debt. You may even be living in a country affected by it. This letter is to address what steps can be taken to abolish it and so I ask you to read it, think about it, and join in the fight for the one true monument to 2000 years of civilization.

The idea I propose is practical, obtainable, and although in my opinion it is the ideal solution, it is far from idealistic. Quite simply, I propose the world's countries and banks should abolish debt to create a new start for people everywhere. I think the first issue we need to deal with is the concept of nationalism.

Every country seems to want to mark the Millennium with a monument, attraction, or party that is bigger and better that its neighbours'. I believe the key to success is to view mankind as one whole race, the human race, and not as individual races. I grant you there are groups of humans different from others, but we are all the same species, any differences being the direct result of evolution to the climate to produce, for example, varying skin colours in different areas. By taking this view, I believe we will overcome the primitive and material nature of humans and progress to greater ideas and beliefs.

So why not combine Millennium efforts towards one whole, big and useful objective? I think that in the middle of the most indebted country we should place one simple sculpture of the world. This will symbolize the joint teamwork by me, you and the rest of the world. After all, why spend all this money on marking 2000 years when it turns out that Jesus was probably born earlier and that we are already into the next Millennium? If the developed world has so much money to throw about, how about showing how much the human race has matured by showing compassion for less fortunate human beings?

So what can be done? Canada has already abolished some debt that was owed to it and others hopefully will follow in their stead. You yourself can do all sorts of things to support this scheme. To make a contribution you could write a letter to your government or sign a petition. One such petition is the Jubilee 2000 Campaign which can be found on the internet at http://www.web.net/~Jubilee/debt.htm#3. Even if the money saved on Millennium projects is not enough, it has been found that banks have the means to abolish the debts. So I urge you to do what you can.

HELEN WALKER, AGED 13

When I grow up I hope that pollution will stop spreading around the world because it can make people ill.

by Jessica Robins age 6 towans.

BROMLEY ROAD INFANT SCHOOL

CARNEY   ALEXANDER   ADAM

MATHEW

I think mummies and daddies should
be good to children.
NATHANIEL MILTON, AGED 6

I don't snatch. I think people should
not snatch.
FAITH PARKER, AGED 6

TAYLOR

I would like it if people didn't
get run over.
OLIVIA CARPENTER, AGED 6

I want everybody to be happy.
LIZ ON, AGED 6

LYDIA

I hope that people listen to each other.
SIMON HOLLETT, AGED 6

I wish there was warm clothes
for everybody.
ANA CARVALLO, AGED 6

STEPHEN

I think children should be allowed
to stay up later.
KIERAN O'HALLORAN, AGED 6

LEE

I wish that everybody had lots of water.
HARRY BELLENBERG, AGED 6

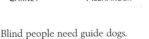
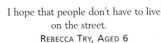

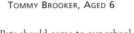

Bromley Road in the future.
We will wear suits with an owl who
has a sparkling solar powered eye.
Our work will be done on our own
fold away computer.
The teacher will be a hologram!
All the boys would have the same
haircut and so would the girls.
We would play lazer controlled games
like chess.
Children will love spinach for lunch!!
We will travel to and from
school in our flying boots.

LUCY ELLIOT, AGED 7

Blind people need guide dogs.
ASHAH PARKES, AGED 6

GABRIELLA

I hope that people don't have to live
on the street.
REBECCA TRY, AGED 6

IAIN

I hope that there will be no more
fighting in the world.
TYLER BRIGHTMORE-COBB, AGED 6

I hope that people don't get hurt.
MILLIE HAYES, AGED 6

AMY

It would be good if people would
be nice.
ALEX WATERHOUSE, AGED 6

I think that people should be kind
to each other.
TOMMY BROOKER, AGED 6

LAUREN

Pets should come to our school.
CRYSTAL WILLIAMS, AGED 6

ROSIE

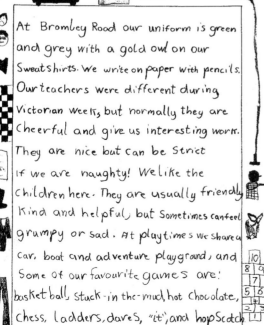

At Bromley Road our uniform is green
and grey with a gold owl on our
sweatshirts. We write on paper with pencils.
Our teachers were different during
Victorian week, but normally they are
cheerful and give us interesting work.
They are nice but can be strict
if we are naughty! We like the
children here. They are usually friendly
kind and helpful, but sometimes can feel
grumpy or sad. At playtimes we share a
car, boat and adventure playground, and
some of our favourite games are:
basketball, stuck-in-the-mud, hot chocolate,
chess, ladders, dares, "it", and hopscotch.
We travel by walking, car, bus, or train, and
are glad to be in the present!

SAM HODGE AND CLASS 2S, AGED 7

I think everyone should help people who are
poor and give them a home.
VICTORIA MOORE, AGED 6

I want that the people that haven't got
any money have some.
JAMIE RAWLINGS, AGED 6

I wish that people picked up the rubbish.
ROMELLE LAWRENCE, AGED 6

I wish that everybody looked after animals.
BILLY TOWNER, AGED 6

I hope that people don't get robbed.
DAVID SHORT, AGED 6

People shouldn't break toys.
ALICE MONIZ, AGED 6

People should have homes.
NATHAN JEFFRIES, AGED 6

KENZIE

JULIET   JASMINE

Every year children celebrate how old
Bromley Road is by having a Victorian
week when Queen Victoria was crowned girls
did not wear bright colours. They wore long pinafores,
aprons, black lace up boots and mop caps.
Boy used to wear flat caps, waistcoats
and short trousers scool children used
to write on slates. In the past teachers used a
cane and a punishment book. we are glad that
teachers have changed! Tin can football.
marbles and hoopla were fun to play. Long ago
children did not have school dinners they used to have
packed lunches instead. They used to walk to school.
Sometimes from far away.

SARAH KIDMAN, AGED 7

LITTLE BLACK NASTY HAT

Now, I am sure you have heard of Little Red Riding Hood, a kind and thoughtful child, but have you met Little Black Nasty Hat? She is totally the opposite. Once upon a summer's day, Little Black Nasty Hat was mucking around in the park, that is to say she was frightening the animals and polluting the environment. She was throwing litter, spraying the playground, and making a mess of the park by pulling up the flowers. She thought she was really funny by doing this, but people thought it was very upsetting and it made their fun in the park really horrible.

One day she was in the park and it was getting dark and foxes were on the hunt for food. She decided it would be funny to trick the foxes. She got a mouse that her cat had brought in the house a day ago and covered it in car oil she had found in the car park. She placed the mouse in front of a fox's burrow, and when a fox came he saw the mouse and went to eat it. The minute it was in the fox's mouth he spat it out and the next thing he knew he was lying in a vet's surgery.

Little Black Nasty Hat's poor mother and sister got many complaints from people and many from the council gardeners. The gardeners were so angry that some moved on to find a new job. Her mother got really fed up when this happened. She tried to stop her daughter from doing these nasty things, but Little Black Nasty Hat just ignored her.

The animals in the park were really unhappy, and some were so scared that they died because their little hearts couldn't cope with the fear they felt when they saw Little Black Nasty Hat. Her mother and sister decided to do something about Little Black Nasty Hat's behaviour and started to do nasty things to her and throw litter and other things into her bedroom. Now, she may have been nasty, but she was extremely neat and tidy. She went absolutely bonkers and pleaded with her mother to stop, but however much she went on at her mother and sister, they just ignored her. The animals thought it was a great idea and decided to join in. They knocked all her books on the floor and brought lots of leaves and twigs into the room. This went on and on for many months. Little Black Nasty Hat pleaded with her mother, sister and even the animals to stop but however much she tried, they still ignored her. Little Black Nasty Hat got ever so upset at this and she couldn't even remember the colour of her own bedroom carpet! She started to feel a little guilty for what she had done but not enough to make her stop her bad behaviour, because if she gave up she thought she would be called a coward and people would think she was a baby. A few weeks later, well two-and-a-half to be exact, Little Black Nasty Hat decided to give up and said sorry to her family and the animals. She also promised to wash the playground she had sprayed until it was shiny and looked as good as new. This took her some time, but when she had finished, it looked so much better and she felt really good for doing it. She started to make friends with the park animals and finally allowed people to have a quiet stroll in the park. She brought food for all her new friends, the animals, and Little Black Nasty Hat and all the animals were happy. For many months she visited her new friends and helped to keep the park clean and tidy.

When winter arrived Little Black Nasty Hat still went to visit her friends, but not as often. She built lots of little shelters for her friends and even took the mice home with her as it was so cold, and she wanted to make sure they survived. She got lots of warm, soft blankets, placed them in front of the heater, and left the mice there to curl up and sleep.

Little Black Nasty Hat really enjoys playing with her friends now, and her friends really enjoy playing with her, and if you ever go and play in the park you just might see her!

CHARLOTTE TOWNSEND

THE THREE GOOD WOLVES AND THE BIG BAD PIGGY

You think you know the story don't you? This is how it really happened!

One day Big Bad Bob (the mean pig) decided he deserved a decent meal, "Fe fo, I feel like a decent meal," he exclaimed. He began to wander round the forest thinking of what he could eat, when he saw three little wolves. Now wolves are known for their stupidity, but these little wolves were particularly bright for their mother and father had been champions at all contests, especially sheep catching, and they had taught their three young wolves the ropes. They had named them Star, Howler and Chaser. Star was the oldest and the brightest, Howler was in the middle and had room for improvement on his brainpower, and the youngest was Chaser, he was fast and didn't know anything. All three wolves lived in a brick house that Star had built.

One day Star was teaching Howler and Chaser how to catch sheep and other animals. As usual, Chaser had run off chasing a butterfly (this is why he was named Chaser). He ran and he ran and he chased and he chased. The butterfly flew out of Chaser's reach and Chaser found that he was lost. He saw Big Bad Bob coming his way and, being the youngest and not knowing how to defend himself, he howled and barked for Howler and Star. They came to him, hot and panting loudly, in about two minutes flat. They also saw Big Bad Bob, but instead of running away or fighting they stood there and let Bob come. He drew closer and said, "I'm going to eat you up! All of you for my supper." "Oh no. Not us!" they pleaded. "Don't make such a fuss!" he answered dismissively. "We simply wanted to say that there is a great Italian down the forest and it's an 'all you can eat' restaurant!" "Oh good. Yipee! I'm so hungry I could eat an elephant!" and off he went. "Such a fool," chuckled Star, "There isn't an Italian restaurant until you get to humanland."

The next day Big Bad Bob came back to complain. "There isn't an Italian down there. You lied to me and now," he said ferociously, "I eat you!" "Wait, wait Bob!" cried Howler. (He had picked up a few tips from the conversation from the day before.) "You can come to our cosy little house and have dinner with us." At this point, with the look on Howler's face, you could just imagine a halo over his head. Big Bad Bob was so hungry that he agreed. When they got to the wolves' house Howler took Star and Chaser into the kitchen. "If Bob is so mean we may be able to change him. If we are nice to him and be his friends then maybe, just maybe, he will change. Kill him with kindness if you will," Howler sniggered. They came out of the kitchen and Star said to Bob, "Feel free to ask for anything." "I'm hungry," moaned Bob, "anything to eat?" "I'm afraid that we haven't been able to go hunting since last week, so all we have are some lambs," apologised Star. "That'll do, but gimmi it now!" he ordered. "OK, as you wish," said Star. Bob ate every single lamb (and the side order that went with it) and so the wolves had to go out to the field called 'Sheep R Us' the next morning. They hunted in the field for an hour. Star caught three sheep and six lambs, Howler caught two sheep and eight lambs, and Chaser only caught two sickly lambs.

They took these back to the house where Bob was still asleep. Star put half the meat onto a huge plate and within ten seconds of the meat being put on the table, Bob was up and eating it. Between mouthfuls he spluttered, "You guys (gulp) are (munch! munch!) the best (gulp)." Star whispered to the others, "Hey that was a good plan, Howler. It's working already!" And it was. For the next few days, Bob said all his 'pleases' and 'thank yous' and started to get better at his table manners. Then they reduced, bit by bit, the amount of food he was getting, but he didn't notice. Bob started to go soft! He wanted to be tucked in at night and started to miss his mummy. "I don't believe it," cried Chaser, "he's gone really soft!"

Star, Howler and Chaser at last said to Bob, "We really like you and we are still friends but you need to go and be independent." "But, but ...," Bob stammered. "You could go back to your home town, Pig City, where your mum is and maybe you could make some new friends," suggested Star. "Well, OK, but if it doesn't work out, can I come back here?" "Of course you can, but you have to try to settle in and be nice to people. Just like you have been to us."

The next day Big Bad Bob packed his bags. Star, Howler and Chaser waved goodbye and, as Bob went, they could have sworn that there was a tear in his eye, as there was in theirs. Bob arrived in Pig City and, yes, he did make new friends and, yes, he did live there happily ever after. The wolves, on the other hand, missed Bob and were miserable for the first week he had gone, but then they got back to their usual routine. Star tried again to teach Howler and Chaser how to catch animals and, for the first time, Chaser didn't run off and eventually got the hang of the hunting game.

That is the real story. That is what really happened.

ABBY CROTHERS

BURNT ASH PRIMARY SCHOOL

HOPES FOR MY BABY BROTHER

Born on June 14th, 1999

My hopes for my baby brother are that he won't go to war, and will live a long happy life, and his hopes and wishes come true.

And that he discovers the thrills of a rollercoaster, or the fun of a water flume.

I hope his name is Sam, and that he grows up intelligent, kind, honest, and that he can stand up for himself.

JAMES LOCKWOOD, AGED 9

TOM MEAD, AGED 5

IN THE YEAR 2000

Robot teachers will use talking blackboards.

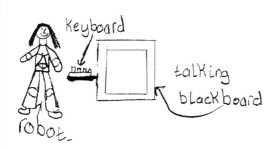

HANNAH CRANE, AGED 8

THE MILLENNIUM BABY

I have a mum and also a dad and my mum is going to have a baby on the 6th October or the 9th October, but there is going to be a lot of work to be done.

I don't want to change any nappies. I don't mind giving milk to the baby. I hope the baby sleeps most of the time. By the way, we don't know if the baby is going to be a boy or a girl. When the baby starts crying, oh the baby will scream, it will be terrifying but we will love it.

I will try to be helpful as much as possible. I might be able to tuck the baby in the cot and sing it a lullaby – if I do, it will be 'Rock-a-bye-baby'.

I will want to push the pram. When the baby starts walking we will have to get the gates down from the loft. We will have to warm up milk for the baby. How long do you think it will take the baby to drink a bottle of milk? I think about four minutes.

STUART LENNON, AGED 7

LOTS OF MILLENNIUM BABIES

JESSICA CAYLESS, AGED 6

The Dome

QASID BHATTI, AGED 5

IN THE FUTURE

Before us all lies the exciting challenge
  of the Millennium
Understanding the world
Reading round the world
Now what will happen?
The Millennium Dome is by the
  River Thames at Greenwich

All parks to stay open for children
  to play
Surprises in store for everyone
How will we get about with roads full
  of traffic jams?

Polite and pleasant people can change
  the world
Robot teachers will use talking
  blackboards
In the Millennium, the Dome will
  open and we hope it will be fun
Make peace not war
All the world to have no rubbish
Racism gone
Youth is our future

Schools will become more high-tech
Can we change the world?
Helping to make the world peaceful
  and happy
One currency, one government, one
  world
Opening the door to the future
Live and let live

CHILDREN OF BURNT ASH, AGED 5–11

CASTLECOMBE PRIMARY SCHOOL

TECHNOLOGY TAKING OVER

AN OLD WOMAN WAS SITTING in her chair using her computer. Technology is taking over. The house was dark and gloomy. The lady stares at the screen, her fingers swiftly pressing the keys. Her eyes seemed to be superglued to the screen. She was shopping, banking and surfing the web. She did everything by computer ... impersonal.

On the other side of the door were three dogs, two of them romping across the grass, the other trying to get the old lady's attention. The lady walked across and closed the black curtains. The dogs were not going to give up.

The next day the old lady got up exceedingly early, she switched on her computer and began typing. She opened her curtains to see the sun and immediately closed them again.

The dogs played in the beautiful park and rolled in the long grass and smelt the flowers. The flowers looked as though they were smiling. The dogs thought of what to do. They decided that they would pick some flowers of all colours, red, yellow, orange and pink. The flowers looked bright. But the problem was how do they get them to the old woman. The biggest dog decided to put them in through the letter box, but they did not look as beautiful as they had done in the garden. Inside the woman sipped her tea. "Oh how I wish the computer would blow up," thought one of the dogs.

The next day it was raining. It trickled down the window pane as if each drop was racing another. She had her computer on all day. The curtains were open. It did not look cheerful in the rain really. But they would

have to try to kill technology once more. Everything they tried, everything they did ... nothing worked.

The next day was sunny so they tried again. One dog stayed inside and clenched his teeth around the curtain and tugged it open, the other two played outside, but she just sipped her tea and carried on typing. She never turned round. She would type the world away. The 21st century was being taken over by technology, or so it seemed. They looked up at the window ... the woman turned round ... but only turned back again. By this time the lady was exhausted. She stood up and stumbled into bed.

The next day the old woman felt very ill, so she stayed in bed. Her bedroom was so gloomy and a gap in the window gave a sharp draught. The walls were once white but were now a dingy, patchy grey. The brown carpet was moulting with age and the grey curtains hid her view of the world. Paint was peeling off the door. The door was by the window through which she could see her garden.

She sat up to see the dogs playing the way she used to play. She used to talk to people and feed the ducks in the park. She had a sudden flashback of memory, leading her back like a path into time. The flowers and the dogs reminded her of how it was in the early nineties. The old woman stood up and started to dance around her bedroom. She sang and danced. She put on her brightest outfit and, for the first time in about nine years, she turned the handle of her door and stepped outside.

She was amazed ... and so were the dogs. It was like it was in the old days, so ... don't let technology take over.

LAURA BUTLER, AGED 11

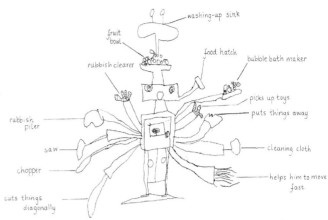

MY ROBOT

I would like a robot like this in the future.
It would keep my house clean and help me lots.
His legs are used as a cupboard.
I can go inside and hide.
He moves by floating.

SHERIDAN PRITCHARD, AGED 6

WISHES FOR THE FUTURE

I wish I could breathe under the water because the ozone layer has got a huge hole in it, and this is causing the sea to rise.

HARRISON MEAD, AGED 9

I wish that all people had homes and food every day. I wish that we could all be friends and live in peace.

SHARMAINE ROWHANI, AGED 7

It would be good if snow was warm but never melted, and it was never cold. It would be good if everyone had a home and was never lonely.

KATIE SHERRY, AGED 10

My wish for 2020 is to be a show jumper. I would like to be a world champion and ride a big, brown horse.

REBECCA RICHARDS, AGED 8

What Do I Want?

I want peace
I want survival
I want love
I want hope
I want a future
I want to endeavour
I don't want fear
I don't want failure
I don't want to be scared
I don't want fighting

REBECCA CLARK, AGED 11

The Millennium

Hopes, dreams, promises, and ambitions,
That's what it's all about.
Dreams for the future,
Hope for the world,
And ambitions to achieve more.
Homeless people have
Dreams that one day their lives will change,
Hope that they will find a home,
Or a warm place for the night,
Promises that they will make their lives
  change and
Ambitions that they will be somewhere better
  next year.
So there's more to life than the
  Millennium Dome.

JESSICA MACKAY, AGED 12

Hope For A New Beginning

The Millennium is coming,
The end of one thousand long years,
We will soon begin another Millennium,
With hopes, ambitions, and fears.

Hope for a new beginning,
Hope to replace all wrong with right,
Hope to live in a peaceful world,
Hope that the future is bright.

Dreams of a world with no problems,
Dreams that the sun will shine each day,
Dreams of a world that is calm and peaceful,
Dreams of a life perfect in every way.

Ambitions for our careers and future,
Fears – will the world blow up like people say?
Ambitions to achieve something wonderful,
Fears – will the Earth fade away?

We all live in this world together,
Let's all go together, hand in hand,
Walking straight into the Millennium,
As if it is another land.

KIRSTY McIVER, AGED 12

What Is Time?

Time is just a way of keeping track,
Of what you are doing.
So what if the Millennium is coming?
The Millennium would be in four years' time,
If someone, whoever it was,
Had started timing our lives
Four years later than they did.
Time is what we, humans, make it.
What if there were 13 months in a year?
The Millennium is an irrelevant thing in my life.

LYDIA HAMILTON, AGED 12

Stop the war's and army uthey's the Police will put you in gaol for evr and evr.

Year 1   Amy Bishop.

I have a dream that teenage crime and prostitution
Is only a figment of an overactive imagination
Instead of a reality;
That drugs and alcohol leave no-one in debt
And dead-end circumstances.

I have a dream where every child is safe in their own home
From every form of hurtful abuse;
That every person is safe to walk any distance
Without a worry of not returning.

I have a dream of no early periods of mourning,
No murder, no need for suicide,
No death from famine in Third Worlds or any other,
That any form of illness can be efficiently treated
In order to save lives.

I have a dream of no racial discrimination
When we all fall from the tree of variety
And land on the soft land we call home as a unit of one;
And when not one animal is exploited,
And that we can have a wider array of opportunity in life.

I have a dream of being able to leave my doors open,
Being able to welcome others into my open house
Without a fear of petty crime;
That there are no damaging wars, just world peace,
No need for any weapons,
Just love, friendship and understanding.

But most of all, I have a dream that every child
Can receive the two most valuable things I do –
Warm love and a good education;
That everyone will give the invaluable love also
And receive the education with open eyes.

I have a dream that one day
These problems addressed can be set straight;
That everyone takes from life all that is offered,
And that everybody dies a happy person.

I only dream of the things that you,
The 21st century children, can change.
Let the mistakes of the 20th century be a lesson,
And work towards a brighter future for all.

LAURA PALMER, AGED 12

I have a dream that one day countries will live in peace and unity,
That one day "Keeping up with the Joneses" won't exist,
That one day our nowadays Hitlers won't want to rule the world,
That our cruel weapons of death, harm and pain will be thrown
    in the fire forever,
That millions of lives will be spared.
And with the hope, help and faith of you, our ancestors of the
    21st century, we can achieve our goals.
With the hope, help and faith of you, the high won't be mighty
    and the poor won't be weak,
And that both will drink and benefit from the same river.
The dream we miss most is that money won't be the root of the tree.

My dream, and that of others, is that all will be respected and equal,
And that you, our ancestors in the 21st century, can and will achieve this.

NATALIE MARKWORTH, AGED 12

I have a dream that one day Black and White
Will be able to walk down the street together with no fear,
Be able to walk and talk like free men.
Let's stop all this fighting,
DO I MAKE MYSELF CLEAR?

EMILY DIPLOCK, AGED 12

MY MILLENNIUM BUG

My Millennium Bug,
He's got teeth the size of a mug,
He's got a cheeky face,
And he leaves no trace,
Of going into our computers!

He's multi-coloured,
And his antennae are flashing.
His tummy is big and bulgy,
Just like a plate of jelly.
Now he's putting on his wellies,
To go into my computer.

He eats the wires like spaghetti.
He gobbles up the mouse,
And leaves the tail till last!
It's going to happen just like the past.
He's got teeth the size of a mug,
That's my Millennium Bug!

KATHERINE EASTWOOD, AGED 9

MESSAGE FOR THE NEXT MILLENNIUM

Men may fight on the Earth and Mars,
Earth may be littered with bottles and cars,
Soldiers will fight with guns and bombs,
Shoeless children may walk on mines,
Animals die from disease and fear,
No food or drink for people so near.
For our future we want something better than this.

Hunger and fear should be aborted,
Everyone working in harmony,
The future is ours – it should be protected
Tomorrow is too late – do something NOW.

ELLIOTT BROOKS, AGED 11

I wish the world would love everyone.
ABIGAIL ALCOCK, AGED 5

I wish everyone was happy, nice and no fighting.
HARRY CROSS, AGED 6

IN THE FUTURE

In the future I don't think there should be zoos because animals should be set free. Elephants should not be killed in order to get their tusks. Bullies should be turned into nice people. I hope that everyone will be friends and people will be like brothers and sisters. I hope there will be no poor people. I would like there to be no more weapons and guns. I definitely hope that there will be no more fighting and that there will be peace in the world. Everyone will be my friend.

SAM SILVESTER, AGED 7

I wish it could be sunny every day in the Millennium so I can play.
CHARLIE SILVESTER, AGED 5

IN THE FUTURE

In the future I would like some people to make headphones that you put on in the morning and plug into the television so that your dream would come up. If you have a Nintendo, you could jump in the television.
I wish that weapons like cannons were not invented and that there will be no wars.
I hope that nobody will be poor and that bullies are made into nice people.

CLAIRE HUGHES, AGED 8

IN THE MILLENNIUM

In the Millennium,
Smoking will be gone,
Rubbish in the bin,
Hunters been and gone.

In the Millennium,
Animals living happily,
Wild and free.
Children playing happily,
Skipping, playing it,
No grazed knees!

In the Millennium,
Birds flying gracefully,
Down, up high,
Troubles been and solved.

In the Millennium,
Good dreams, no bad ones,
Illnesses cured and gone,
In the Millennium.

NANCY SLOAN, AGED 9

Many celebrations will take place,

It's exciting for all the human race.

Lots of changes will occur, both good and bad,

Landmarks will be built, fun will be had.

Electrical products may come to a halt,

New things will be taught.

Now as we approach this new era,

Inventions will be made to make life easier.

Unknown are some things that lie ahead,

Millennium is coming, shall we be glad or dread?

SARAH UNWIN, AGED 11

My New Millennium Invention

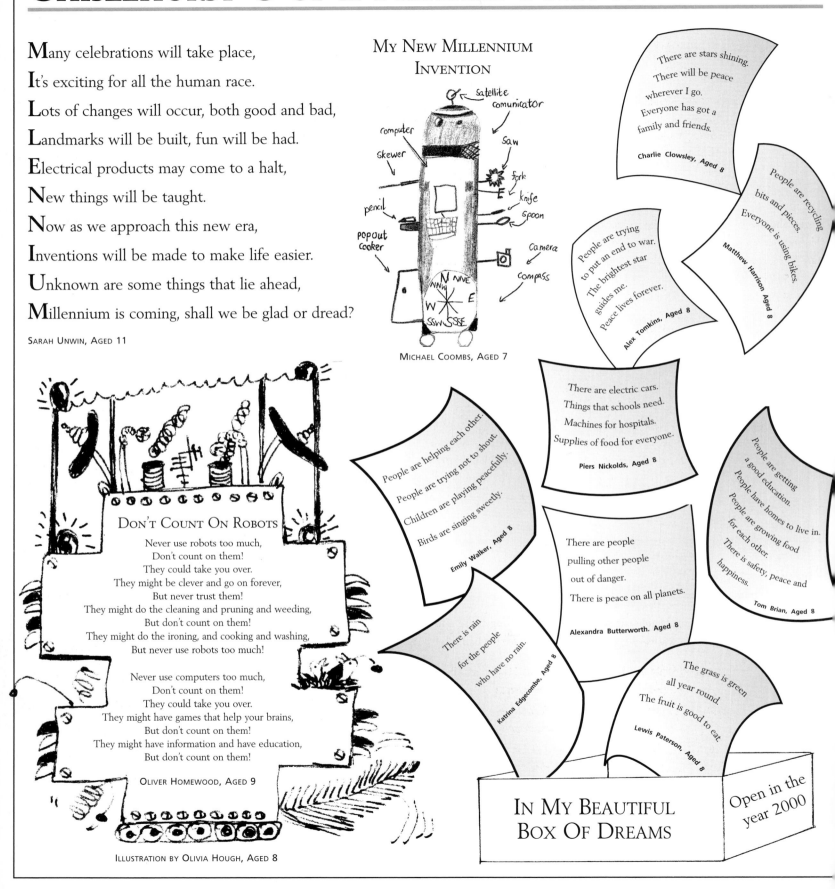

satellite comunicator

computer

skewer

saw

fork

pencil

knife

spoon

popout cooker

camera

compass

MICHAEL COOMBS, AGED 7

There are stars shining.
There will be peace
wherever I go.
Everyone has got a
family and friends.

Charlie Clowsley, Aged 8

People are recycling
bits and pieces.
Everyone is using bikes.

Matthew Harrison Aged 8

People are trying
to put an end to war.
The brightest star
guides me.
Peace lives forever.

Alex Tomkins, Aged 8

There are electric cars.
Things that schools need.
Machines for hospitals.
Supplies of food for everyone.

Piers Nickolds, Aged 8

People are helping each other.
People are trying not to shout.
Children are playing peacefully.
Birds are singing sweetly.

Emily Walker, Aged 8

People are getting
a good education.
People have homes to live in.
People are growing food
for each other.
There is safety, peace and
happiness.

Tom Brian, Aged 8

There are people
pulling other people
out of danger.
There is peace on all planets.

Alexandra Butterworth. Aged 8

There is rain
for the people
who have no rain.

Katrina Edgecombe, Aged 8

The grass is green
all year round.
The fruit is good to eat.

Lewis Paterson, Aged 8

Don't Count On Robots

Never use robots too much,
Don't count on them!
They could take you over.
They might be clever and go on forever,
But never trust them!
They might do the cleaning and pruning and weeding,
But don't count on them!
They might do the ironing, and cooking and washing,
But never use robots too much!

Never use computers too much,
Don't count on them!
They could take you over.
They might have games that help your brains,
But don't count on them!
They might have information and have education,
But don't count on them!

OLIVER HOMEWOOD, AGED 9

ILLUSTRATION BY OLIVIA HOUGH, AGED 8

In My Beautiful Box Of Dreams

Open in the year 2000

CLARE HOUSE PRIMARY SCHOOL

HOW AGOUTI GOT PALE BROWN FUR

ONCE LONG LONG AGO, in Zimbabwe, there was a cunning young leopard. He was eight years old, a teenager in leopard ages. He lived in a hole in the longest tree in the African continent, but he spent most of his time in the shade hanging or sleeping on top of a long, brown branch.

One day he was racing at his fastest speed, 70 miles per hour, when he skidded to a halt, he heard "HELP! Anybody!" He ran to the place where the voice echoed from. There on the dry jungle floor was a huge, golden eagle. She was so terrified that she suddenly fainted in leopard's paws. He put her on his back and they sped to the big tree. Leopard got some hay, leaves and bark and put her on it. Then he found a hunter's camp blanket and put it on her. Next day she woke up and said, "My name is Tsipporah. I live in a tree. Unfortunately a lion scratched my left wing. I was so terrified I fainted." Leopard said, "Do not worry, you will be safe here." And she was. She played with him, she slept with him, she even ate with him, and they helped each other catch their prey.

But one day a jealous, but greedy, Agouti came to live in a mountain bush opposite. He was very jealous of leopard's fur. So, in the night he stole leopard's fur and he swapped it for his fur. Leopard roared when he saw himself in the morning, so Tsipporah decided to help. "This is my plan," said Tsipporah, "Well, you know he loves food? Well, we can set out a food trap. We put mountains of food outside his house and when he is in a lazy sleep we steal his fur." So they did it, and he never stole again.

AVA LLOYD, AGED 7

FLORES THE KNIGHT

LONG, LONG AGO there was a knight called Flores who lived in a palace. He always had to fight dragons, he was very kind, the King chose him to be his dragon knight. He was very good at fighting dragons. He had fought 100 dragons before he was tired of fighting dragons. He couldn't go home otherwise the King would have his head. So, one day, he ran away.

Soon he found himself having a very burned bottom. A dragon was frying him on a pan, frying him up and down. Then Flores jumped off the pan and the dragon said, "I will only not eat you if you kill all your knights and your King and your Queen and your Queen's baby." When he got home he didn't kill his friends who were the knights. And he didn't kill his Queen either, and he didn't kill his Lord Thomas either. "If I did kill him, I would be killed," he thought. So one day he went to the dragon's house. He took his sword and he killed the dragon.

JAMES JARRETT, AGED 6

CRIME DOESN'T PAY

It was one of those nights where everyone stays inside tucked up by the fire, everyone except Robber Robinson, that is. He was down in his cellar making some very important plans.

Also, just on the other side of town, a police officer was leaving work to go home. He was a bit down in the dumps because he had knocked tea all over his work. When he was nearly home, a piece of paper blew out of a window and landed at his feet.

"Goodness me, what's this then?" he cried. He found out Robber Robinson was planning to destroy the Millennium Dome. He phoned the police and they arrested Robber Robinson straight away. He was put in jail for a long time.

"Crime doesn't pay!" said the police officer.

REBECCA HEATON, AGED 8

THE SPIDER AND THE ANTS

ONCE UPON A TIME, three ants who were part of the 17th colony discovered a plot to destroy the bug world was being hatched by a mysterious insect, known only as 'the Millennium Bug'. The three ants, whose names were Speck, Dot and Itch, decided to launch a rescue mission, and held a council to decide where the animals should hide from the Millennium Bug.

They decided on either The Millennium Dome or Birmingham NEC. They voted and the results were: Millennium Dome 72%, Birmingham NEC 28%.

The animals started to move along towards the Dome, with more than two million animals and insects following them. A spider ushered them on saying things like, "Don't delay, if you don't hurry it'll be May."

The animals trekked on, assisted by more able animals. The cheetahs carried the storks, and snakes were carried by eagles. After two months the animals finally reached their destination. They were then told by the owl leader that the Millennium Bug did not exist.

Moral: Check your facts before you act!

JEFFERSON REGAN, AGED 11

MILLENNIUM

Stop air pollution
Make electric cars
Stop people being homeless
Help us learn
Help us read
In poor countries
Stop people starving
We want these things
To help people survive
and live in happiness

BARNABY YAU, AGED 7

THANK YOU GOD FOR FRIENDS

EMMA BRASSINGTON, AGED 7

I hope that animals are
looked after.

TANYA OSMAN, AGED 5

DEAR GOD

We will get fresh food for you to share.
Help us to look after the world.

ALEX HALL, AGED 5

MILLENNIUM PRAYER

Dear God,

Make the world nice.
Help other countries to get more food.
Help other countries to get money like us.
Help us and other people.
Help the trees to grow in this world.
Help us to love each other.
Help boys when they are men
so they can get married.
Help the tooth fairy to get the tooth.
Help hot countries to have water.
Help people to have birds to have eggs.

Amen.

LOUIS DAVIES, AGED 6

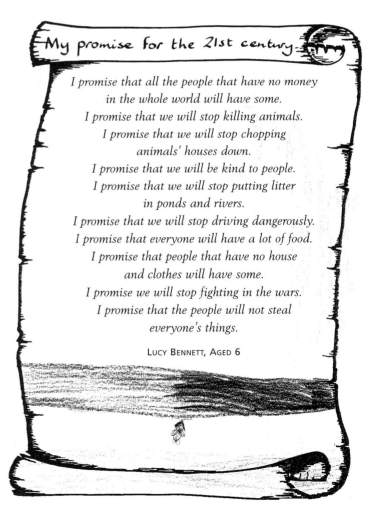

My promise for the 21st century

I promise that all the people that have no money
in the whole world will have some.
I promise that we will stop killing animals.
I promise that we will stop chopping
animals' houses down.
I promise that we will be kind to people.
I promise that we will stop putting litter
in ponds and rivers.
I promise that we will stop driving dangerously.
I promise that everyone will have a lot of food.
I promise that people that have no house
and clothes will have some.
I promise we will stop fighting in the wars.
I promise that the people will not steal
everyone's things.

LUCY BENNETT, AGED 6

THOUGHTS FOR THE NEW MILLENNIUM

I WISH ...

for animals to be respected by humans

KEELY

there was less pollution

LUKE

that people would start recycling
more paper and glass

AIMEE

that people would stop fighting

GEORGINA

there was a cure for cancer

SCOTT

that there was better technology
for everyone

CRAIG

that people would stop throwing
litter into the sea

JORDEN

that everyone will be able to
enjoy themselves!

PENNY

that poor people had seeds and water

JAMES R

that I could play snooker and
work at the same time

JACK

that people would stop killing children

KAYLEIGH

for a free world

KIRSTIE

I HOPE ...

people will stop cutting down trees

DANIELLE

it is a beautiful world

SOPHIE

they will invent a rocket backpack
for old people

GRANT

everybody will look after the world

MAXINE

that there will be better
security systems

JOE

I WISH ALL CHILDREN ...

had a teddy to cuddle

CHARLOTTE

could have houses to live in to
keep them warm

BLAKE

had blue houses

MOLLIE

could have millions of toys

CHEZNEY

had clean water to drink

FRANKIE

had clothes because they will
get wet and cold

JOEL

I WOULD LIKE ...

to have a calm world

HOLLIE

to be a policeman

TOM

the world to be snowy so I can
make snowmen

LOUISE

no more crime

PAUL

all the people to have food to
make them strong

JAMES M

all of the poor people to have fruit

RYAN H

to clear up the world and
make it beautiful

MARK

all wars to end

LOUISE

a wonderful, kind, and
peaceful world

RYAN

lots of trees with blossom on

JAMES C

people to care about animals

REBECCA

people to look after the rainforest

HANNAH

THE 2000 WISH

ENOUGH FOOD · NO POVERTY · HAPPINESS · NO FIGHTING · NO TRAIN OR CAR CRASHES

MY FAMILY HAPPY AND HEALTHY · NO MILLENNIUM BUG · NO KILLING · ALL VISIT THE MILLENNIUM DOME · NO WAR IN KOSOVA AND WORLD PEACE.

NO PEOPLE · NO RACISM · HOMELESS · CURE CANCER · CURE THE HIV VIRUS · PEOPLE ALL LOVING & CARING

I want to be a ballerina

When I am bigger I will be able to have a house of my own.

I will be a vet I will look after animals who are sick and poorly. I will make them better.

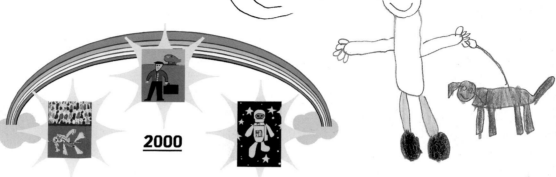

2000

I will be a museum keeper.

When I am bigger I will be a policeman.

Changes

Now I am six I can ride a bike. I would like to change people being a bully. I would like to be a illustrater.

DARRICK WOOD JUNIOR SCHOOL

FREE THE ANIMALS

I hope that every child and grown-up in the world will have a proper house, clean water and healthy food to eat. I hope that no animals will be poisoned, shot or trapped in those traps with sharp zigzag teeth. I hope there will be no people who throw plastic bags and plastic bottles in the countryside and into the sea and pollute it.

RACHEL BOYD, AGED 8

CURE ALL

I hope that all the disabilities of our world will be solved by a cure that a doctor invents for the new 1,000 years. All the diseases will disappear and all the homeless and lonely people will be as happy as us.

VICTORIA ROBINSON, AGED 8

THE DREADED MILLENNIUM BUG

Tick Tock, Tick Tock
10, 9, 8, 7, 6, 5, 4, 3, 2, 1, 0, zzzz.
That's the sound of the countdown to the Millennium on the TV. If you're wondering what the zzzz is, well, it's the TV going blank just like the computers, CD players, radio control, plane radios and fire alarms. If there is a fire will the fire brigade know? More importantly, will you know? Will the computer IDs be wiped out? Chaos everywhere. What will happen to you? So it's not Happy Millennium, it's watch out!

DANIELLE HOWARD, AGED 9

SARAH JANE'S MILLENNIUM WISH

My wish for the Millennium would be to see people walking more often, and for people to put their rubbish in the bin, not any other place. I also want everyone to look after the animals if they're in danger.

SARAH JANE SMITTEN, AGED 8

I wish that everybody could be free and have a free life because they could experience new things.

ROBERT LAKE, AGED 8

POEM FOR THE MILLENNIUM

No more fighting,
No more war,
Getting rid of 'Hitlers'
Forever more.

Blast off
Into space,
A far-off destination,
A united place,
For all the nation.
Just a pleasant
And green land,
Built for recreation.

Make sure
Acid rain
Never comes again.
If we work together,
Pollution will
Be a thing of the past,
But how long will it last?

ALEXA DOWNING, AGED 11

My Thoughts for The Millennium

The Millennium,
a next 1000 years.
There shoudn't be tears.
The world should be peaceful,
full of animals and trees,
foxes and bees.
No wars or fears.

Will there be pollution?
Will there be clean air?
Why will it be so different,
from this 1000 years?

JAMES MARTIN, AGED 9

VICTORIA'S TIME CAPSULE

VICTORIA CUNNINGHAM, AGED 12

VIDEO: *I would put in a video showing lots of historical events, such as world wars, the sinking of The Titanic, new inventions, etc. I would also put in a video of the Kings and Queens and Royal Family so they could see what they wore and what they were like.*

DICTIONARY: *I would put a dictionary in so they can see our language and compare their words with ours. They could also see how many words mean the same thing.*

MONEY: *I would put money in to show people what kind of currency we used. I would put some old 10p's and new 10p's in so they can see how it has changed.*

MAP: *I would put in a map of London and a map of the whole of England, so people can see what places looked like when we were alive and how much it could have changed by the time they saw the map.*

PHOTOGRAPHS: *I would put in a photo album or a collection of photos from someone's life so people could see what we did and had to face.*

SCHOOL BOOKS: *I would put in school books to show how we used to learn and what we used to learn. It could show them new things that might have been forgotten and how hard or easy our world was.*

2000

A Poem of Consequences

The truth be known-
We're dying.
We're drowning in sorrow
And lying.
We cannot find,
The truth behind,
Deception and
Corruption.
When the world fell,
into our hands,
We stole the wealth
from the land.
We banished all purity,
Lost all beauty,
And discovered a world
of destruction.
The future should hold
A better destiny.
Fate mustn't cross
The line of reality.
You're our only hope -
The future must cope,
With the consequences
Of our insanity.

CHARLOTTE RUSSELL, AGED 14

LAST CHANCE

So much has happened
But so little gained
So many people have fought
Fought through hope, reality and pain

Help for the future
These people are our family
They need our aid
They need security and love money cannot buy

How hard they try
To better themselves and be free
So it is now our duty
To take this chance and free their souls

We must praise those who have fought
Let them lead us on our path of duty
We must take this chance to try
Let's attempt for a possible peace

Let's all lend a helping hand
Remember every little helps
Every prayer and every word
We must continue on this long road to recovery

Always remember this chance
Remember your contribution
For it comes just once every 1000 years
Once the day is over the chance may be lost

AMY TOGHILL, AGED 13

Millennium Poem

The streets are crowded now,
The traffic is very slow
Traffic lights have changed
From red to green,
now the cars can go!

It won't be like that in the future,
Cars will fly in the air,
Parking won't be a crime
There'll be space everywhere.

Hospitals are crowded
Waiting lists are long,
There are too many diseases
Soon we'll all be gone.

It won't be like that in the future,
There'll be lots of people around,
People won't die of diseases
cures have all been found.

Earth is over populated
Pollution is killing man,
Wildlife is dying
We are running out of land.

It won't be like that in the future
When men live on the moon,
Jupiter too, and mars,
We'll need the future — soon.

KATY DENTON, AGED 13

MAKEDA THOMAS, AGED 6

THE LEOPARD WHO LOST HIS SPOTS

We all know leopards have spots. Well this story is about a leopard who didn't.

There once was a greedy leopard. His name was Sammy. Sammy got so fat his spots fell off. All his friends laughed at him. The next day all Sammy's friends saw how sad Sammy was. That night when Sammy was in bed all his friends were busy making some spots.

The next day all of Sammy's friends gave Sammy the spots they made. Sammy was happy. Sammy said, "I've got spots again!"

They played and played. Sammy and his friends had a very, very good time.

The End.

SONNY COCHRANE, AGED 6

DAISY MEAGER, AGED 7

PETER HOPKIN, AGED 6

TIASA DEY, AGED 6

Downe Primary School

Millennium

Mystery was the natural world when Darwin came along,
Investigating and exploring far distant lands.
Labelling and noting everything he found,
Living creatures examined accurately,
Evolution laid out for everyone to see,
Nature viewed in a different way.
Now we begin to look into the future,
Imagining a world, one always changing,
Unknown – animals altering,
Mankind evolving.

YEAR 6, AGED 11

A Prayer For A New Age

Dear God,
I pray all trees will not be destroyed.
I hope people will not pollute.
I trust people will not kill.
I wish crime will be stopped.
I would like to hold the Earth.
I will try to protect the Earth.
Amen.

YEAR 4, AGED 9

Millennium Wish

I wish for people to stop selling guns.
I wish there were no poachers, and they would stop killing animals for their skins.
I wish that people would stop cutting down the rainforest.
I wish that nobody needed to sleep on the streets, and all people had enough money for food and drink.
I wish that people didn't feel sick and then die.
I wish it would stop.

YEARS 1 AND 2, AGED 6–7

A Better World
Our Wish For The Future

I would like to make another ozone layer.
I hope there will be world peace.
I pray that all the people in the world live happily one day soon.
I hope the extinction of animals will stop.
I would like people that are starving to have food.
I will try to help all animals and plants which are dying.
I hope homeless people find homes.
I wish that racism will stop.
I wish that there would be more sharing in the world, and people would be satisfied with what they have got.
I will try to make the world a better place,
I wish to find out what is the meaning of life?

YEARS 3, 4 AND 5, AGED 8–10

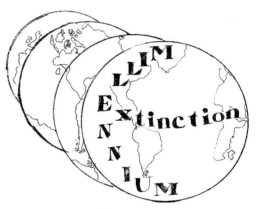

Thoughts On The Dome

Magical, mystical Millennium Dome,
I feel as if I'm in a heavenly home.
Lovely sparkling lights in the night,
Looking down from such a great height.
Elegant dancers on a flashing stage,
Now go in, whatever your age.
Never before has there been one of these domes,
It's got a museum with dinosaur bones.
Unusual things are in this building,
Many exciting, magical wonderful things.

YEAR 4, AGED 9

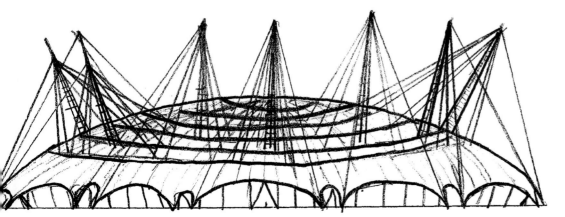

Millennium people listen up
I've got some things to say
Let your world be better than in my day
Let deforestation stop
Encourage people not to chop
Not to destroy and
Not to invade
Invading American Indians was wrong, so
Undo the misdeeds we have done
Millennium people there's work to be done

JENNIFER YIELDING, AGED 10

THE 20TH CENTURY

We've invented the telephone,
Discovered flight, and made the Dome.
We've been to the Moon,
Flown around the world in a hot air balloon,
And someone designed the television.
We made up cricket and learned division.
I can't pronounce Millennium,
Instead I say Minnellium.
We've killed people,
"Coz they're an enemy."
We've done all this,
And much, much more,
All in the 20th century.

THOMAS PURDIE, AGED 10

OZONE HOLE

The ozone layer has been spoiled
It makes me feel like I've been boiled
The sun's so hot
The wind so cold
It feels like I've been controlled

LOUISA BUDD, AGED 10

A PRAYER FOR THE 21ST CENTURY

Dear God,

Help us preserve the trees and not take them for granted. Assist us to plant new ones and not cut too many down. When we use paper encourage us not to waste it or throw it away. Help us to think before we do things so we won't make a mistake and do anything silly.

Amen.

JOSEPH TEBBS-WARNER, AGED 10

I wish.....
that Kosovo didn't have the war and they had more food and they had lovely toys.

JACK GREEN, AGED 6

I wish...
that in the Millennium no more people would fight or start a war because honest people are being killed. I wish that in the Millennium people would stop putting chemicals in food because people could die.

MICHAEL PILKINGTON, AGED 7

I wish...
that in the Millennium we will stop blood sports and killing for fur because we won't have many animals left. Stop smoking because it can make you die and it hurts your heart and lungs. Stop fighting in the wars because it is sad when someone dies.

NICOLA GANDER, AGED 7

1000 Years to come

Cars that hover,
Rich people live on our moon,
Robots work for you,
and they use convertable spoons!

Inflatable houses you can carry around,
Animals can talk,
Chat with people on Tv,
And finally fishes can walk!

You can take things out of The T.V.
Animals are treated like gods,
Trains can fly up to the sky,
And babies are born in pods!

People have long Luxurious tails,
Dragons and unicorns are well known pets.
Tigers and wolves run wild through the woods,
And jelly fish chomp through marshmallow nets!

by Katie, Tsai, Larua and Alice.

FARNBOROUGH PRIMARY SCHOOL

ALANNA HUGHES, AGED 8

ANOTHER YEAR OLDER
BLOW OUT THE CANDLES AND MAKE A WISH!

I am the world and this is my party!
I will blow out the candles and make wishes for my future!
1... 2... 3...
I wish that I had a machine that could go back in time,
When war did not exist – not even for one day!
Everyone would then be happy.
I long to be filled with happiness, kindness, goodness and honesty.
I wish that my people could live together and be friends forever.
I wish that people would stop hunting and killing my animals
  – please leave them alone!
My animals should not be trapped in cages: let them be free.
You should be proud of such wonderful creatures!
I wish that people would start to realise how much damage
  is being done to me.
Please stop dumping oil and waste in my crystal-clear seas.
Please don't drop litter: bins were made to be used!
Protect the environment.
I wish that, in the future, people could still see the beauty in me!
Just imagine a world without the glory of nature: only made of stone
  – How dull that would be!
Well, you have heard my wishes; I hope they come true!

YEAR 3, AGED 7–8

OUR PROMISES

Dear World,
Our promises are to love our world and care for others.
We shall try our best to do a good turn every day
  by not hurting people or making their lives difficult.
We promise to make our world a peaceful, relaxing place
  and put an end to hating.
If we do something wrong we should tell the truth.
We would like every child to have a good, loving home.
We promise to make the world cleaner and to stop polluting
  the environment.
We would like the poor to have enough food to eat.
And if we work together, we can make the world a better place!

YEAR 4, AGED 8–9

THREE CHEERS FOR OUR BEAUTIFUL WORLD

Fragrant flowers,
Tall trees,
Red roses,
Shimmering sun,
Radiant rainbows,
Cotton wool clouds,
Salty seas,
Magical moon,
Shining stars and
Amazing animals.

Three cheers for our beautiful world,
Hip! Hip! Hooray!
Hip! Hip! Hooray!
Hip! Hip! Hooray!
We hope its beauty is here to stay!

RECEPTION CLASS, AGED 4–5

A LITTLE WISH

The past is war,
The present is destruction,
The future is peace,
The future is Earth.

A little wish for the future:
For there to be peace,
Peace on Earth,
For friendship to come upon us.

I wish that wars would end,
The start of a new trend.
I wish that people would start
To give the environment a thought.

I wish, I wish, I wish, I wish ...
Is there any point in this, I wonder?

YEAR 5, AGED 9–10

SAVE THE BEST 'N' FORGET THE REST

I want to save the world!
I don't want people crying anymore,
I don't want bombs and fighting,
No more war.
I want to save the world!

Forget punching and pushing,
Forget illness and hunger,
Start caring for each other,
I want to save the world!

YEAR 1, AGED 5–6

More money to go around.
Illnesses cured.
Love in the hearts of everyone.
Laughter heard everywhere.
Enjoy living on Earth.
Never let people down.
No more hate and hurting.
Ignorance to be stopped.
Unite countries for a peaceful world.
Mankind must change its attitude.

Millennium ... let there be a change!

YEAR 6, AGED 10–11

MILLENNIUM MAGIC

If I had a magic wand,
Do you know what I would do?
I'd wish that all people were kind to one another,
Let's start with me and you!

If I had a magic wand,
Do you know what I would do?
I'd wish that no-one in the world was ill,
And were healthy like me and you!

YEAR 2, AGED 6–7

Every
member
of our school
signed our shield.

Friendship

Love

No wars

Happiness

WE HAD A DREAM

*We had a dream that in the year 2000,
it would be a beautiful world where
children and adults would be safe.
There would be no such thing as pollution
and there would be no litter dumped
anywhere. There would be a world of peace
with no fighting or arguing. Towns and
countryside will be looked after regularly.*

*The world would be a place of happiness and
you will hear children's laughter on every corner you turn.
The birds will be singing peaceful melodies in every season.
That is the dream we have and we dream
that all children should be able to
experience a dream of happiness.*

TANYA NICHOLLS AND
REKHA BEGUM,
AGED 14

Peace

No hunger

THE RUBBISH BOY

One cold, rainy, blustery day long ago in Wales, there was a boy called Dave. He was filthy and he was disgusting. He thought that he was very smart but Dave never ever put rubbish in the bin. Dave's mum called him the rubbish boy.

"Oh you are so untidy, so scraggy, so dirty and filthy," sighed his mum. He was out in the garden while his mum was talking. He dug a big deep hole into the ground. Then Dave went back indoors and got his mum's picnic basket and lots and lots of food for himself. Dave was quite greedy so he loved picnics. He ate it all in half an hour. There were five huge, gigantic, enormous and tall mountains of rubbish. He went inside again and got all of the rubbish that he dropped. There was so much rubbish that it made another mountain and then ... Ugh, oh, all six mountains fell on him and he never got sick again.

Moral: Be careful, take care of our planet because this could happen to you!

HARRY KENT, AGED 7

HAYLEY CHAN, AGED 8

"When I am a grown up I want paper and bottles to be recycled."

ASHLEIGH WILSON, AGED 5

A PRAYER FOR PEACE IN THE YEAR 2000

Dear Lord,
Can we have peace throughout the whole world. For races who are against each other to embrace each other in friendship. For neighbours to love one another and for rich people to help the poor. Dear Lord, can all the children in the world have a good education so we can all have the same opportunities in life. For all parents in the world to love and care for their children. May all the world be a neater and happier place for everyone in the new Millennium.
Amen.

HAYLEY WORF, AGED 8

LEAH'S HOPES FOR THE FUTURE

In the future I hope there are no more wars. Be kind and loving to people. Make the world clean and safe. Please make the poor happy and give them nice homes and better places to live. Please give them money. Please give them a lot of money. Please help us make the world a better place for people.

LEAH BASSETT, AGED 7

PROMISE FOR THE 21ST CENTURY

In the 21st century I would like to see no more trees cut down because without trees there would be no more air and we would die! It makes me feel sad because the animals have nowhere to live.

In the 21st century I would like the government to stop destroying forests because all the animals have nowhere to live and sometimes they run across the road and get killed. The way we could do this is by not throwing away old wood. Instead, you could take your thing made of wood apart and use it again.

MICHAEL BOND, AGED 9

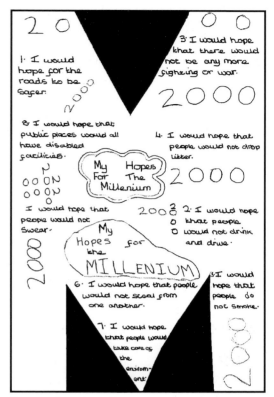

KATHERINE CRISP, AGED 10

THE KIND PERSON

One night last week, John decided to go for a walk. He hadn't had much exercise lately. He thought a walk would do him good. John was West Indian, he had moved to England four years ago. He picked up a torch, put on his black padded coat and set off.

The woods were quiet and there was little movement. It was a beautiful moonlit night so he didn't need a torch. He walked for hours and hours. He was thinking about going home when he saw a blur. Then he was knocked to the ground; he was unconscious.

When he woke up the birds were singing. He tried to get up but he couldn't. He groaned. Then he heard thumping feet. It was the priest. Relief entered John.

"At last," he thought. "At last." The priest just walked past John. "Never going to your church again!" thought John angrily.

About an hour later a teacher came along but again he walked past at a rapid pace. So John was left lying there. When another person came along John had no hope, but to his surprise he knelt down and took John to hospital on his motorbike.

The hospital was lovely, and the nurses were kind. His doctor, Dr Smith, said he didn't need an operation. John got lots of 'Get Well' cards.

When John got out of hospital and was watching the news, he saw the person who robbed him. He watched on. "This criminal has been put in jail for 15 years for assaulting John Hooper," announced the news reporter. "His name is Bradley Allen."

From that day John went swimming for exercise instead of walking. He thought it would be much safer.

Moral: Don't be racist.

YEAR 5, AGED 9–10

HANNAH'S PROMISE FOR THE 21ST CENTURY

Some poor people in different countries don't have food or water. It never rains there so they can't grow crops to eat. It makes me feel awful when I pick up some food and think about them. I think it's unfair that we've got lots of schools and they've got none. My promise for the Millennium would be to raise lots of money and send it off to countries that really need it.

HANNAH PAYNE, AGED 9

HAWES DOWN INFANT SCHOOL

CHARLIE'S WISH

My wish is for everybody to have an education and to get a good job.

My wish is for the richer people to give the poorer people money so that they can get more homes and schools. It will also help them to get the food and water that they need.

My wish is for people to look after the world and not to put pollution in the seas and in people's houses, and not to put rubbish on the floor and not to give other people germs.

CHARLIE CROCKWELL, AGED 6

RACHEL'S WISH

In the year 2000 I would like all children to go to school because they need to learn how to read and write.

I would also like people to put rubbish in the bin because the world will not smell.

I would like people to not kill animals because the animals will not be seen again.

I think people should share what they have because some people have nothing. Some people have lots of things.

RACHEL MUNNS, AGED 6

APRIL'S WISH ....

Everyone to have a big smile on their face and enough toys to play with.

APRIL O'FLAHERTY, AGED 5

I wish that people would pick up their litter and put it in the bin and the world would be a cleaner place.

TONY DAVIES, AGED 6

I wish that people would not destroy the world.

JACK SELFE, AGED 6

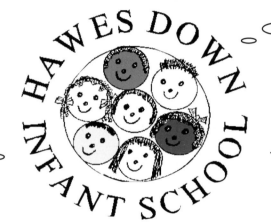

I wish that everybody could be nice.

BLU FRANCIS, AGED 5

I wish everyone has their own wishing star.

JENNIFER SWEENEY, AGED 6

OUR WISHES FOR THE NEW MILLENNIUM

To make the world a more colourful place by planting flowers and then taking very good care of them.

Everybody will smile at their friends and family and we will all be cheerful.

We will all be kind and helpful to other people.

RECEPTION CLASS, AGED 4–5

MILLENNIUM

Make us grow
In the sun
Like a tree
Like a flower
Everyone grow
Night and day
Night and morning
In the rain
Under the sky
Make us grow

RECEPTION CLASS, AGED 4–5

CHRISTOPHER'S WISH

I think animals should not be killed, like elephants. People kill an elephant to get the elephant's tusks. I'm a loving person and a caring person. When I grow up I don't want to kill animals. I will help them and care for them. I am going to be a doctor when I grow up.

CHRISTOPHER JOHNSON, AGED 7

ZOE'S WISH

My wish for the next Millennium would be for everybody to be healthy. I would also like for people not to die through their illness. There should be more cures.

My wish for the next Millennium would be for everybody to have lots of money and to have lots of things like us. I would also like for everybody to have drinks of water and food. In other countries like Northern Africa I would like for all children to have drinks and food because they have not got them. I would also like them to have clothes and homes. We have homes so the people in other countries should.

My wish for the next Millennium would be for people to have education like ours. The children in Mozambique don't have any schools so I would like to help by collecting cans.

ZOE CROUCH, AGED 7

Hawes Down Junior School

Learning In The Future

In the future I think teachers might be robots. The robot would have a screen on her/his face. It would have sums. I think that when you press a button on your desk a computer could pop up so that you could do your work. I think in your desk there would be CDs. I think that every pupil will have a mini spiky robot of their own. It will have two long arms and six wheels. If you have finished your work and you want to play you can press a button which makes a Playstation pop up.

THOMAS PENNYCOTT, AGED 8

Future design for the Millennium Dome

CHRISTOPHER REAVELL, AGED 11

All Change, No Change

Tomorrow will be a different year,
A different century, a different
Millennium, but it will be no different to
The day I speak in, the day today.

Tomorrow I will be a different person,
A different human, a different child, but
I will look no different from the child
I am, the child I'm speaking from.

Tomorrow I will grow a different plant,
With a different seed, with a different
Leaf, but it will be the same plant,
The same plant I grew this day.

Tomorrow I will have a different feeling,
With a different touch, with a
Different meaning, but it will be the
Feeling, the same feeling I felt this day.

DENISE BENSON, AGED 11

2000

For me the inspiration of life
Is life itself.
Learning, developing, and growing
In knowledge, as each year passes by.

From being a baby I have grown just like
The wise old owl, and the Earth itself.

We look back over 2000 years
At war, disasters, and tragedy
And then turn to the future
And hope it fades away.

Throughout night and day mankind
Learns in many different ways.
And I would like the future to be full of peace
Where people become friends
Like the silence of the planets in the sky.

The Millennium is a new beginning of our future.

JOSHUA STRATFORD, AGED 11

The Millennium Window

There was once a Millennium window
Hidden away in the corner of a room.

A schoolboy looked through the window
And saw himself not being bullied.

A policeman looked through the window
And saw no trouble on the streets.

A doctor looked through the window
And saw a cure for cancer.

A journalist looked through the window
And saw nothing bad happening anywhere.

A mother looked through the window
And saw a happy family.

God looked through the window
And saw hope.

CHRISTINA GREENSLADE, AGED 9

RICH, POOR AND MONEY
A FABLE FOR THE MILLENNIUM

Once there was a tiger called Poor. He lived in an African jungle. Also in the jungle, lived two lions called Money and Rich, and these two were brothers.

One day, Money spotted Poor looking very downcast and thin. He realised that the tiger had not enough to eat and drink. He thought of the meal that was awaiting him and hurried on.

A few days later, Rich noticed Poor looking even thinner and more unhappy than when Money had seen him. He, too, realised that the tiger needed help. He remembered the big meal he had just had, and felt pity for the creature. He made himself acquainted with Poor. He gave him a big meal and soon the tiger was looking healthier than he ever had before.

A few weeks passed. One day, Money saw Rich and Poor talking together. He remembered, with a pang of guilt, how he had left the tiger on his own. He went over and apologised for his selfishness. Poor forgave him and soon all three of them were laughing and playing together.

Moral: Help people in poverty and the world will be a better place.

MAIA LASK, AGED 10

THE BOASTY HARE

Boasting hare thinks he's fast,
So challenges a tortoise.
He shoots off like a whirlwind,
Then stops to have a rest.
Tortoise plods to the finish,
Boasty Hare loses.

Moral: Slow and steady wins the race.

STEPHEN CRAWLEY, AGED 9

ACHIEVING PEACE
A FABLE

There was once a group of native Americans who lived on one side of the River Stickes. The cowboys lived on the other side of the river. They fought for five years over who the river belonged to.
Over the years some of the Native Americans and some of the cowboys were killed. They still argued about who the river belonged to.
One day the Native American chief asked to talk with the cowboy leader.
They decided to share the river after that.

Moral: If they had talked to begin with, no-one would have died and there would have been peace.

JAMES RICE, AGED 8

A Message For The Millennium

In the 21st century will you be living on a different planet? Or are
you already? Is your TV a computer or a table or a microwave? In the
21st century are you going to be friends with Aliens? Is a light bulb
an oven, is all this to be found? Is peace around? Are animals in cages?
Are people and animals roaming free?

HAYES SCHOOL

ONE STEP CLOSER

Millions of people joining hands,
Ingenious ideas across the land.
Laughter fills the air around.
Lights are seen and love is found.
Excitement is felt everywhere.
Not knowing whether it will be the end.
It's a chance to start again,
Undo the past and make amends,
Make the world a better place and
   keep a hold of our human race.

LEILA ARAGHI, AGED 14

NUMBERS

The world is a bright, neon sign.
The sky is an intense snapshot of colours,
Competing for the limelight,
Fighting for their own fame.
The air is heavy with excitement,
Anticipation and scepticism.
The news and affairs are forgotten as people
  dance and laugh.
Carefree for now, while the fear is left behind.
The present is the past,
The future is here.
The planet for a moment loses itself,
Numbers and dates are thrown to the wind,
The sound of fun is deafening, comforting,
  familiar.
The Millennium is here.
She watches in amazement as the sky
  explodes with colour,
She listens with hunger to fun and
  freedom expressed in the deafening din,
She sees the world, glowing, dancing,
  laughing,
She knows the night is here.

LOUISE MCKENNA, AGED 14

CENTURY

The end of the year is upon us,
It is like the end of an era,
To those who have lived and died,
Will this be an extinction of a life?
2000 years have passed us by,
The old and the young,
Asking questions, like, Why?
A new century approaches us,
The Millennium, a time for all emotions,
Of happiness, sadness
And thoughts for those
Not so fortunate to enter this new life.
A time where friends, families and enemies
All join together.
To welcome the future,
To say goodbye to the past.

The Millennium, a time
To forget the bad,
And to remain with the good.
A time to say goodbye to those who have died,
To look to the place above,
Where they lie now,
Welcoming the life of new beginnings.
The party poppers pop,
The music plays loud.
To be heard,
Are the screams and shouts
Of the new Millennium
And all the good it brings.

JENNIE CRISP, AGED 14

THE DREAM

Think of the things that the future holds,
That we may never see.
We don't know what will happen next,
We don't know what will be.
We don't understand the future, it's not ours to tell.
We know it's the end of an era, we know when
  to tell.
Maybe a new beginning, to life as we know,
I hope an end to tragedy, will begin to show.
Why everything can't be peaceful, I just don't know.
Why people are so cruel these days,
I can't tell.
I hope the Millennium will be good,
I know it will be, I know it should.
Time and money have been spent
On creating an amazing event.
Light the fireworks tonight, so
Everybody will catch the light
Of hope, of love, of peace sometime.
Pour out the booze, let's have a good time,
Sing songs, dance away, make peace here to stay.
So let's hope everything goes right,
And let's celebrate throughout the night.

PHILIP CROSSINGHAM, AGED 14

MILLENNIUM

The Millennium, it's here at last,
Time to celebrate and forget the past.
Everyone's out partying, all having fun,
Nothing really matters, what's done is done.
Now's the time to start again,
Forget our enemies, make new friends.
As the clock strikes 12 o'clock,
Most people are happy, some still in shock.
Adults are drunk, kids are screaming,
Some people hardly believing.
In 2000 years we have gained a lot,
Some of which will all be forgot.
How much longer will we be here,
When will it end?
Will another Millennium come round again?

JENNIE MORRISON, AGED 14

Highfield Infant School

My Millennium Wish

A magic chair would have wheels and it would take me to school.

Jessica, Aged 6

My teacher will be a robot. I will press buttons.

Alexander, Aged 6

At lunchtime there will be a menu. You can tell the invention what you want. I'd still want a double chocolate cookie and a mars bar.

Sarah, Aged 6

You can make a spell to get dressed. A robot does your teeth for you. When you go to school you go in a rocket and watch TV all day.

Chloe, Aged 6

I would come to school by computer. I would press Enter and I would be there just like that.

Henry, Aged 5

Everyone would have a computer on the table.

Freddie, Aged 6

My wish for the next Millennium is to stop the wars by talking to one another. War is bad because it brings more problems in the world.

Joe, Aged 6

Emily, Aged 4

There will be no teachers in school, they will be robots.

Ben, Aged 6

At lunch there will be metal trays because the dinner ladies are going to be robots.

Jordanne, Aged 6

I would come to school on my bed with wheels and a computer that I could play on.

Christopher, Aged 6

I would like to go on a flying bed so I could sleep on it all the time.

Laura, Aged 6

I would travel in a frisby. I will drive myself.

Timothy, Aged 6

I hope people will look after their pets properly. I want to set up a pet service to look after people's pets while they go to school or work.

Rachel, Aged 7

People should try not to build so many buildings in place of the fields, because it spoils the wildlife and the animals go away.

Laurence, Aged 7

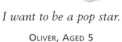

I want to be a pop star.

Oliver, Aged 5

I will travel in a rocket. My dad will drive it. I will look at the stars on the way.

Timothy, Aged 6

I want to be a swimming teacher.

Amber, Aged 5

I would like to invent a packet of pills. If you eat the pills it will make you speak any language. If I had these pills now I would be able to speak to my grandmother in German.

Emily, Aged 7

I would travel in a fish tail that I would have at home. I would put it on and it would take me there in a flash.

Helen, Aged 6

My food will float to me with a control.

Russell, Aged 6

I would like to invent a bubble that goes around you so that you can still do anything you like outside.

Grace, Aged 7

Highfield Junior School

Tiger, Tiger

My wish for the 21st century,
  is to save the tiger from extinction.
It is a beautifully, brightly coloured animal,
  and, it is under threat.
Most of this problem,
  is caused by poaching.
They are killing the tigers for their furs,
  and bones for medicine.
It's illegal.
It's wrong.
And it shouldn't be done.
I hope the tiger survives.
I hope there will be no problems.
I hope that my wish comes true.
We cannot afford to make yet another animal,
  fade away like this.
At this rate,
  by the next Millennium,
  the tiger will be no more.
And yet,
  if we try,
  we can save it.

Jennifer Garrett, Aged 10

Dear Lord,

The sky, the wind, the sea, the rain,
Help us to care for them once again.
The owls, the moon, the stars at night,
The little firefly glowing bright.
The dancing, pink and yellow flowers,
Which hang and bloom on swaying bowers.
The gentle, softly singing whale,
The peacock with his elaborate tail.
The wild mustangs running free,
This is the land I wish to see.
We listened, but did not understand,
What God said when he made our land.
Please show us what's right and how to follow your way,

I pray it will continue day after day.

Amen

Charlotte Gray, Aged 10

Millennium

When the Millennium comes
My wish would be
To reduce the amount of smoky
  pollution,
So we can help people with asthma
  and other diseases.
To care for people who live in
  countries
Where there is hardly any food or
  water.
To prevent people
Cutting down trees
That help us breathe.
Help keep lakes
Clean as crystal.
Keep the air fresh,
From all germs that surround us.
If these suggestions are made,
The world will be a better place.

Luke Withecombe, Aged 9

I Wish

I wish that we could breathe
Fresher cleaner air.
I wish that the sea
Could be used as
A nice place to swim,
Not a private dumping ground.
I wish that people would stop whale
  killing,
Just leave them to swim free.
I wish that people would use the bins,
Instead of the pavement and road.
I wish people would stop laying
Main roads through the countryside,
Because it is destroying animals' homes.

Bret Austin, Aged 10

A Dodgy 2000 Poem

In the year 2000 there will be ...
A computer in place of me.

My home will be a zooming rocket
With a computer in my pocket.
Right then school will be ...
A minor part of me.

But what about the teachers?
I don't know!
We'll just have to wait and see ...
War will end, peace will be
And we'll be looking in virtual reality.

Hopefully a serious matter
Not to laugh and not to shatter.
Because this new Millennium brings
Lots of goods and less of the bads
To make a poor person glad.

Jacob Taylor, Aged 9

What We Need

My Millennium experience will be fun.
I hope never ending wars will stop.
Love and care for lonely people.
Let's hope the planet will change.
End poverty, a fairer share of wealth and food,
  not just for rich people, poor people too.
No more wars, co-operation, that's what we need.
I hope illnesses which we are not able to cure,
  can be cured.
Under my skin, deep down within
My Millennium experience,
I hope the world will change to be a happy
  place again.

Jessica Cleary, Aged 9

THE HIGHWAY PRIMARY SCHOOL

DISASTER!

What shall happen, what shall we do?
Why can't the computers cope
with something new?
Will the clocks and phones crash?
Under the table we shall clash!
Will the aliens invade?
Arm yourselves with
the garden spade!
Will something slimy
climb up the loo?
What shall happen, what shall we do?

EMMA RICHARDSON, AGED 10

DEAR GOD

When we wake up in the 21st century we would like to see the flowers alive and beautiful nature outside, the Sun shining with beautiful countryside. When I wake up in the 21st century I would like to see a loving family of ducks still in the pond, and streams and rivers still flowing. Thank you, please make it come true.

When I wake in the 21st century I would like to see the world all healthy with thoughtful families, the schools teaching children and feeding them with healthy food. I would like to see mothers caring and all families healthy.

We could not live in a world of pollution or with very little nature. Think what we have now and keep hoping that it will be the same in the 21st century. Let us love what we have got.

Amen

GEORGIE ROWELL, AGED 8

SMOKE

Through it everybody suffers,
Him and her run for their puffers,
Everybody knows it's bad,
Oh really, it is quite sad.
Factories come, shoot out smoke
On everyone, it makes them choke.
No-one knows that they are nasty,
But ...
Everybody knows they're ghastly!

DOUGLAS HARRIS, AGED 8

MILLENNIUM POEM

Mucky air being turned clean,
Incredibly nice people, not mean,
Lovely, peaceful, quiet, happy,
Love the unwanted, teach the happy.
Eternal laughter, lasting long,
No more sewage, dirty water gone,
Never again will people strike evil,
Ice cold wine and cakes with treacle.
Utter rudeness will never be thought of,
Millennium celebrations filled with love.

PRAYER

Wildlife should come to land,
Birds should sing out loud,
It's a new day,
Alleluia, alleluia.
Animals running around,
Alleluia, alleluia.
Birds singing in the trees,
Alleluia, alleluia.

LEWIS FOOT, AGED 8

A BIGGER SLICE

My mummy made some cakes for we had a picnic in the garden because it was a sunny day. There were three cakes on the plate – I had one and my brother had one. We both wanted the last cake. We shouted, and when we looked down the plate was empty and Sara the dog was licking her lips.

CAYLA RILEY AND
REBECCA WELCH, AGED 5

THE EMPEROR PENGUIN AND THE POLAR BEAR

On a cold and windy day there was a family of Emperor penguins all fishing. They caught four fish and then they all went back for one more. While they were fishing a polar bear came and took all the fish. He rushed back to his den. He was in such a hurry he slipped on the ice and lost all the fish. Because the polar bear was lazy and greedy he had to stay hungry.

SIMON FANNER AND
NEIL BANNISTER, AGED 7

POLLUTION

Rivers are being treated like bins,
I think you might find a crisp packet on the beach.
Vast amounts of rubbish are being dumped,
Extinction, it is getting nearer every day.
Rivers are homes to wildlife, which is dying,
So I think we should think about where we are putting our rubbish.

ROBERT GREGORY, AGED 8

MILLENNIUM

Magical world without any fear,
In the sea and rivers crystal clear,
Lovely forests coming back to
Life to live for
Eternity.
New buds sprouting, on old trees,
Never to be cut down in this world.
I want this world to be
Unbelievably natural in the new
Millennium of two thousand.

STEPHEN KIMPTON, AGED 11

MY PROMISE

My promise for the future is that there will be no more war when the 21st century comes. I want no more because thousands of refugees have had to flee their homes to get away from the fighting. I wish for peace.

ELLIE HOUGH-HILL, AGED 9

I HOPE

I hope that people will stop killing animals for fur coats. They just want furs to make them look posh. Do they know that each fur coat is wiping out species of animals? The reason I chose this is because I like animals and I enjoy their company. I just wish there were more.

KATY DENNIS, AGED 9

I LONG FOR A FUTURE ...

Where beautiful birds can carry on
   cheeping,
Where daring dogs can carry on
   barking.

Where perfumed flowers can carry on
   growing,
Where bending branches can lean
   for birds and insects.

Where graceful spiders can carry
   on spinning their webs,
Where shiny black ants can crawl
   in no danger.

Where insects can nest peacefully and
Where gigantic gnats can flutter about.

Where red, spotted ladybirds can
   fly without fear,
Where crumpled up leaves can blow
   in the wind.

Where silken petals of roses can slip
   through your fingers,
Where smooth leaves can glide
   gracefully in the midsummer air.

Where sticky goosegrass can hide
   in the hedgerow,
Where brightly coloured bees can
   buzz around freely.

That's what I long for.

LAUREN REID, AGED 10

I long for the beautiful sweet smell of lavender,
The scent of the wonderful, delicate pink rose,
The smell of newly cut green grass.

I long for the feel of tough goose grass,
The silky touch of a wild flower bud,
The roughness of the brown copper beech
beneath my fingers.

I long for the birds to sing a song,
The wind to rustle the leaves in the tree tops,
The grass to swish in the soft spring breeze.

I long for golden irises to curtain themselves
in the long green reeds,
The shiny black ants to silently crawl,
The fluffy dandelion clocks to sway in the wind.

LILY JARDINE, AGED 10

I long for a future of birds and bees,
For wasps to pollinate the bright, perfumed trees.

I long for a future, it can't be wrong,
For birds to sing their distinctive songs.

I long for a future of shiny ants,
For daisies and luminous buttercups so bright.

I long for a future of glowing blue skies,
For the wind to rustle the leaves so high.

OLIVER NELSON, AGED 9

Where fresh perfumed flowers grow,
Where birds gather sticks, flying fast, high
   and low,
With the smell of fresh lavender all around,
And ants nests like sandy volcanoes there on
   the ground.

I long for a future where the grass is a shining,
   emerald green,
And where miniature minibeasts can be seen.
I hope the sky stays a light, fiery blue,
With bright buttercups and daisies
   reproducing new.

I long for a future with shimmering trees,
And for people to appreciate the work of
   the bees.

LAURA BARTON, AGED 10

Where bright yellow bees can buzz amongst
the flowers,
Where blackbirds can sweetly sing their song,
Where the crow's black, sleek feathers can ruffle
with delight,
And where the graceful ants can build their
complex nests.

I long for a future with fresh spring flowers,
With silver birch trees that sparkle in the sunlight,
With their rough, ragged trunks,
And leaves blowing breezily up to the sky.

I long for a future that way.

LEAH MOSS, AGED 10

MAY ...

May flowers dance in the fresh, cool breeze,
May birds stride in the soft, green grass,
May spiders hang from their silken webs,
May flies nest on the edges of leaves,
May insects scamper to their nests,
May the birch tree sparkle in the sun,
May the smell of lavender fill the air,
May the dew drops form upon the ground.

GEMMA PETKEN, AGED 10

May the leaves still spray out like the glistening water from a fountain,
May the birch still stand like a sword of silver,
May the roots of trees still claw through the earth like bones of a hand,
May the black shiny ants still scurry through the pathway of the gnarled
   old trees,
May the grass still grow like a blanket carpeting the ground on which
   we walk,
May ...

MEGAN BENTLEY, AGED 10

ILLUSTRATION BY
CARLOS CARRILLO, AGED 10

MILLENNIUM 2000

DURING THIS MILLENNIUM we have discovered and seen some very amazing things, like new medicine, new inventions and lots more. We have also seen some very bad things, like unfortunate deaths, crashes and wars. All of the families who have experienced these bad things know how it feels to lose a family member or friend, so I hope that in the next Millennium, no-one will kill anyone and everyone will just live in peace.

At least we have good things to live with, not just bad things. Patients with diseases can now be cured, thanks to the new technology that doctors can use, fires can be put out thanks to the equipment that firefighters use, and people can be rescued from places like dangerous cliffs, thanks to inventions like helicopters and grabbing hooks, plus a lot of crew that use these inventions who are also needed.

In the future there will probably be more ways of curing people, or even ways to stop them from getting ill or hurt in the first place. This is very likely since they have already invented robots that can explore inside of doctors. I also hope that pollution will be reduced by recycling glass and papers as well as using non-polluting cars.

Personally, I think that if thousands of us would work together we could stop crime and make the Earth an even better, cleaner place than it is at the moment. We could help the disabled and unfortunate by giving them technology so they could get on with their own lives by themselves, like we can. Then if someone becomes injured or hurt there will be more people to help cure that person.

Recently we have all been working pretty hard to make the Earth better, but we all have to work extra hard to make it a perfect world.

SAM COX, AGED 10

MESSAGE TO THE FUTURE

Dear Somebody
I hope that in the future every person has food and somewhere to live.

MARK WHITE, AGED 6

GEORGINA WATKIN, AGED 8

THE MILLENNIUM

The Millennium makes
me think of different cars
coming down the road.

The Millennium makes
me think of Prince Charles
becoming the King
of England.

The Millennium makes
me think of more roads
being built.

The Millennium
makes me think of
more rockets going
to the Moon.

The Millennium
makes me think
of different roller
coasters being
built.

DANIELA FORZONI, AGED 5

MESSAGE TO THE FUTURE

I am writing this from the year 2000,
To those who live in the year 3000.
Right now there are wars which I don't understand,
People dying every day and no help is at hand.
I deeply hope that by now you've found peace,
With all the killing and bombing ceased.
I also hope the homeless are homed,
Away from the streets which they've wearily roamed.
The blind see light and the deaf hear sound,
The dumb speak and the lame walk around.
Please don't forget the important things in life,
Your friends and family, your husband or wife.
Keep them close to your heart, love them as they've loved you,
For one day they'll be gone, and you will be too.

HELENA FERREIRA, AGED 12

Whatever your future may hold
Say my prayer as it is told:
Lord, help everyone in this generation
And may you keep us as one big nation.
Amen.

STACEY SULLIVAN, AGED 12

RECIPE FOR THE FUTURE!

100g of happiness,
200g of love,
50g of peace on earth,
70g of joy and hugs,
A tablespoon of sugar to
sweeten things up,
A cup full of heaven –
Bake for 100 years until
soft and fluffy.

CARLY MAIRS, AGED 12

MILLENNIUM BUG

ZOE QUINN, AGED 15

MESSAGES TO THE FUTURE

I close my eyes, and far away,
I'm dreaming of another day,
Where stars fade out, and wishes fall,
To be granted for one and all.

And what may be of what's to come?
What of laughter, what of fun?
Dictators, governments, hells of fire,
Love washed out with all desires?

Angels dancing as we run through
clouds,
We climb further up and we'll never
look down.
Moving forward to the future, the
new day to come,
But will it be filled with peace and
with fun?

MARY PUDDLE, AGED 13

Will every mobile phone used be "radiation free"?
Will every pupil in a classroom have a lap-top PC?
Will technology get the better of us,
As we stride for greater power?
Will someone invent the flying bus,
Or perhaps a robotic flower?

NATALIE WHITWORTH, AGED 15

A message for the future

I wish people wouldn't go in their cars so much. So they can get fit and the air won't be so dirty.

by Debbie Gayle. Age 6 $\frac{1}{4}$

James Dixon Primary School

In 100 Years' Time

There will be talking photographs
There will be shoes to let you walk
on water
There will be flying taxis
There will be pencils that draw
what you tell them to
Everybody will be able to whistle
nice music

RECEPTION CLASS, AGED 4–5

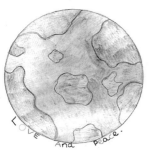

*If we work together we can have
a great world!*

Changes For The Millennium

... not hunting wild animals
... not cutting down trees ... cutting down on cars
... more policemen and women
... more schools in poor countries
... more people helping the poor
... more traffic lights and islands
... less air traffic delays
... more school clothes shops

... no more wars

YEAR 3, AGED 7–8

Inventions For The Future

... an information pen. When I press a button it gives me information so I can get on with my work.

... my super rocket paramedic. It goes fast and it zooms. It will save more people's lives than ever before.

My wish is that the factories will not pollute the air and water.

I would invent an alarm to go off if they pollute the air and water.

YEAR 2, AGED 6–7

In The Millennium

*I would like to go to Space
to see the planets
I think there will be lots of
rockets for me to go in.
I would like to help the
Aliens mend their satellites.*

YEAR 1, AGED 5–6

In 30 or 40 Years' Time

Televisions won't be like they are now. We will have mats and when you tap on them the programme you want will come up. When the programme has finished you will be able to pick up the mat and walk away with it.

YEAR 5, AGED 9–10

Hopes And Dreams For The Future

To the leaders of countries on Planet Earth:

Let us have the chance to build solar machinery and solar powered cars which cut down pollution. Let us do all we can to combat litter. Give us a chance to do it!

Together we could all explore space. If we find anything new then we could declare it everybody's and share whatever we find.

Think about all the good people of the world and the good that they do and have done; people like the Red Cross, the Salvation Army and the NSPCC.

Let us tear down all the skyscrapers and flats so we can build big cottages. There won't be any more small and horrible houses.

We could do more for the homeless. We can build new houses, give them furniture, food and drink, and also give them clothes to wear.

We could do more to combat illness like cancer and AIDS.

Let us build a food tube to Africa so we can feed the people there more easily.

We are all different. That's what makes us special. We should learn to appreciate that difference.

YEAR 4, AGED 8–9

Imagine ...

Imagine if there were no
cars being driven in traffic jams.
Imagine if we all had something to eat
and no one was homeless.
Imagine if there were no weapons to
harm or kill people.
Imagine a world where everyone shared
and no-one was selfish.
Imagine if there was no fighting, nothing
to make you cry.
Imagine if there was peace where we
could all rest.
Imagine flying taxis and a running bus,
Cars that run on water and plants that
live on us!
TVs that are 3D and telephones with
surround sound,
Skateboards that hover and aeroplanes
on the ground.
In the year 2000 things are going to
be cool.

The things that ruin our world today are
rubbish and burning fuel.

Imagine flying toasters, swimming bees,
walking fish and money trees.
Imagine singing hoovers, barking cats,
jumping elephants and purple rats.
Imagine clever sheep, three-eyed frogs,
giant people and mooing dogs.

Imagine warm ice, fire that's cold,
Imagine if we never grew old.
All these things I'd like to see,
In the year 2000, in space I'd like to be.

CLASS 6, AGED 10–11

LONDON 2050

Some of the students wrote their visions of what London would be like in 50 years' time. Some wrote about how it could be if we act wisely; others wrote about how it might be if we continue to act unwisely. These are some of the best bits.

THE HEADACHE

At 8.30am the alarm sounded again: "Jack! Get up!" it barked, waking him with a start. He lay in the dim light, not remembering who he was. His head throbbed horribly. Then realisation flashed into his mind.

"Oh no," he moaned, "I'm late!" A stream of images flooded his mind: the endless dole queues; his fight for employment; the puffy-red, angry face of his boss as she fired yet another "malingerer". With a surge of anxiety he leapt out of bed. As his feet hit the floor, an immense pain crashed through his head, making him dizzily crumple on the carpet. He didn't know what was happening. He had been having headaches for a few months, but nothing as severe as this. Jack struggled to his feet. He looked at the clock: the illuminated glow of the numbers read 8.45am. He stumbled around, panic stricken, trying to get ready. "Lights." The lights came on instantly with a humming noise that made him feel sick. "Off," he hissed through clenched teeth. Then another chunk of memory came back: it was Friday, the day he worked from home. He almost collapsed with relief. There was no need to rush today. As long as he was logged-on by 9.30am, nobody would realise that he was ill.

When he felt confident enough, he stumbled out of the bedroom to the living room, where he stood using the doorframe for support. His head felt like it was made of lead. His headache was so bad that he could hear the blood surging around his cranium with every heartbeat. His living room was a blur. He forced his eyes to come into focus. He saw an antique Ikea coffee table littered with take-away cartons, coffee cups and CDs. Stumbling with haste, he made his way over to the coffee table, knocking all the CDs on to the floor, uncovering his new Sony lap-top. He pressed the connect button and typed in the word 'Hospital'. After a pause of 20 seconds a message appeared requesting him to type in his National Identification Number.

Another wave of nauseating pain broke in his head. The screen turned a pale green colour and he saw a Red Cross logo in the top left hand corner signifying that he was now at the NHS site. The currents of nausea swelled as he tried to focus. He clicked on the 'Symptoms' button and then punched in the key words that matched his symptoms: headaches, dizziness, nausea, memory loss and disorientation. He closed his eyes as he waited for the diagnosis, realising for the first time that he was scared. He had never been ill. It was so unreasonable! What was wrong with him? He prayed that it would

be something that would not force him to take time off work. He opened his eyes. The words 'URGENT! Your appointment is at 10.45am. Click to confirm' flashed in red letters on the screen. The bad dream was turning into a nightmare!

"Mr Thornton!" bellowed a voice from a concealed speaker, jerking Jack out of his stupor and echoing along the empty hospital corridors. "Dr Adams will see you now." He was confronted with a grey-haired woman sitting behind a very old wooden desk. The doctor was viewing Jack's medical records on an equally ancient I-Mac that was perched on top of the desk. To his right he could see a newly cut lawn with beautiful rows of flowers that neatly ran along the edge of the grass. It would have been a pleasant view but for the large hospital sign on the opposite lawn. The woman at the desk pointed to a chair. "Come and sit down, Mr Thornton."

The doctor scrutinised him as though he were a strange and rare specimen. Her voice sounded almost excited. "Am I right? You have been getting very bad headaches, dizzy spells and feeling nauseous ...," she quoted the rest of the list of symptoms that he had keyed in earlier that morning. Jack nodded, too nervous to speak. "In that case, the first thing we need to do is give you a brain scan." The doctor said this as if he had just made her day. Jack didn't like her tone at all. The doctor saw the confused look on Jack's face and explained in an authoritative and self-satisfied manner, "I don't want to be alarmist, but we think there is a possibility that you may have a brain tumour." She pressed a button on the intercom. "Nurse, please escort Mr Thornton to the scanning room." The nurse came in almost instantly. He led the dazed patient out.

Jack sat by the phone all day, feeling as scared as he'd ever been in his whole life. He had been told to go home and wait. Someone would be in touch that day with his scan results. When the phone rang that evening, Jack was so anxious that he nearly knocked it off the table. "Hello, Mr Thornton." It was the voice of Dr Adams. "As we suspected, you have a malignant tumour in your brain."

Jack's vision clouded. He could feel a tear rolling down his cheek. The doctor's voice continued even though he was no longer listening. "You will have to come into the hospital for two days next week. The treatment is complicated, but we have a 100% success rate. It's really nothing to worry about." Jack's mind was stunned. How would he ever manage to get two whole days off work?

RICHARD MARSHALL

A DARK GREY SKY hangs above London like an eagle watching its prey. A pigeon flies away from the city and soon disappears from sight in the thick air. A tall sky-scraper tries to break free from the choking, sulphurous smog that creeps in every day. There is a crackle and roar of lightning and the rain starts to pour down on the city like a shower of ash.

The thick, bruised clouds keep out the daylight. You can see that the capital is gridlocked by slow-moving traffic. The rumble of engines and HGVs mingles with the drum roll of thunder from the sky. Car horns blare as drivers vent their frustrations.

It is hard to breathe the polluted air. Everyone is rushing to find shelter from the dirty acidic rain. Most people wear breath masks.

The buildings are black with soot. Even the newer buildings are covered with a layer of dirt and grime. All windows and doors are firmly closed. Looking carefully at the wide doorway of a shopping mall you notice that it has inner and outer doors like an airlock to keep the polluted air out.

Regent's Park is still there, but the trees are all dead and bare, the grass is black and withered and the ponds are empty. The statue of *Eros* above Piccadilly Circus is blistered and eroded. He casts his sad gaze across what was once a busy centre of social activity. Today it is desolate and empty. Even the pigeons have gone. The city is a diamond brooch on an emerald cushion. A thousand sparkling

surfaces reflect the light of the brilliant sun beating down from the cloudless, azure sky.

It is as though three million bees are all crowded into one shared hive. A constant drone and buzz of activity rises up through the clean air. The city is a beautiful, spring flower, open to the bees.

A glass tower glistens in the sun like an ice sculpture. Inside you can see the tiny figures of workers, like termites, in the chambers and galleries of a giant nest. On the side of the building you can see row upon row of solar panels, absorbing the sun's energy to power the building's systems. Looking around you can see that all the buildings have a carapace of solar panels glinting in the sun.

The roads that are the veins and arteries of the city are less crowded than they used to be in the 20th century. Taxis queue by busy stations, the diesel rattle of yesteryear replaced by the soft hum of their electric motors. Private cars drain smoothly into underground car parks at the edge of the city centre. Motorcycles zoom around like flies. Buses manoeuvre efficiently around the capital in their own bus lanes. Trams roll down the thronging city streets.

Now that the centre of London has been pedestrianised there are loads of open-air cafés and restaurants thronging with people enjoying the mid-day sun. Many more stroll along the wide streets, through the parks, or simply laze by fountains, relaxed by the silvery sound of the running water.

DANIEL PRICE, ROBERT REINKE, CHARLES LIKI, SCOTT ROWLAND, TONY DRISCOLL AND DANIEL MOVAHEDI

EARTH PRAYERS

Oh maker of land that was green and lush,
You made the mountains and you built the trees,
You created the eagle and the rivers that rush,
I pray to you now down on my knees.
Pollution and toxins are killing our Earth:
The planet's a factory, now brown not green.
Maybe you could give it a new birth,
Because what it needs is a big spring clean.
The Earth you made was once like Heaven
Can we have that again in the next Millennium?

JONATHAN BELSHAW

Heavenly Father,
Thank you for my life, my family and friends. Thank you for the green grass, the blue skyand the brown soil.

Thank you for forgiving us for polluting and destroying the world you made. We're sorry, but as the saying goes, "You don't know what you've got until it's gone."

IAN RUGYENDO

Mathew,
Aged 13

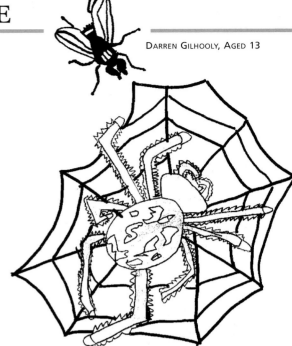

Darren Gilhooly, Aged 13

The Elephant And The Mouse

An Elephant called Nelly was walking through the jungle when she saw an ugly Mouse and started to scream out loud. The Mouse looked up at the Elephant and then Nelly said, "No wonder nobody likes mice because they're so ugly."

The Mouse said, "No wonder nobody likes elephants because they're so huge and fat."

The Mouse began to cry and so did the Elephant and they both ran away. The next day they met up again (not deliberately) and they both looked away as if they had not seen one another. But then Nelly the Elephant saw a peanut by the Mouse's foot and she ran as fast as she could, just missing the Mouse. She grabbed the peanut and she said to the Mouse, "Would you like to share this with me?"

The Mouse replied, "Whoooo meeee?"

"Of course you silly. Who else is here?"

And the Mouse then replied, "Oh, OK then."

They enjoyed the peanut and from then on they never called each other horrible names again.

Moral: Accept the looks of other people and think about their feelings.

Perry James Simmons, Aged 13

The Spider And The Fly

There was once a fly that flew around thinking he wouldn't ever be caught. But one day he almost flew into a spider's web. He kept making the spider angry by saying, "You can't catch me." The spider got very angry and then the fly got very sleepy. He accidentally flew into the web and the spider ate him!

Moral: Don't take things for granted and don't be over-confident.

Ryan Lee, Aged 13

Harry J Wilson, Aged 13

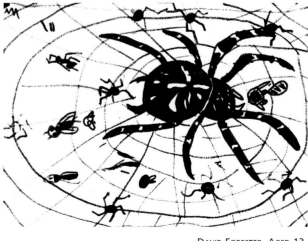

David Forester, Aged 13

Keston

Our school is great fun because on Thursdays we do art and craft and sometimes we do cooking and make all sorts of things. On Friday the class does country dancing and I love country dancing. Sometimes we go on outings. Soon we are going to go to Broadstairs. You can go in the sea if you bring your swimming things.

MOLLY PATRICK, AGED 7

In the New Millennium I hope that I hope the school will still be here with the woods around it.

SIMON BENNETT, AGED 5

Looking Back And Looking Forward

IN THE LAST MILLENNIUM, man has done good and bad things – things like wars and starvation, but also good things like art and good inventions. Take Thomas Edison. If it wasn't for him, New Year's Eve wouldn't be bright and colourful with lights.

Man has also done a lot of bad things, like the Second World War. This all started because of Hitler's hate of the Jewish race and his want for Germany to be Europe's super power. There have been other wars too, like the First World War, the Falklands War and the Gulf War.

There have been bad things too that were not caused by man, like disease, hunger and famine, which have all been caused by the environment. But there have also been bad inventions, like the atomic bomb and pollution.

Man hasn't been bad all through the last Millennium. There has been good too. If it wasn't for Ferdinand Magellan, we might still think the world was flat, and if it wasn't for James Cook, we wouldn't know about Australia and New Zealand. If he hadn't mapped Australia, lots of explorers would have been wrecked on the Great Barrier Reef. If the Victorian Age had not happened, we wouldn't have the telephone or lots of other good inventions like the toilet that flushes.

Throughout this Millennium, architecture has changed, got better and probably also sometimes got worse. There have also been phenomenal buildings like the temples built by the Aztecs and the Egyptians, as well as the great temples built by the Romans and Greeks and the massive castles built by the English and French.

I think for the first few years of the new Millennium not much will change from the way we live now. There may be a sudden breakthrough like a pill or some medicine that could make you live longer than you can now. But I think there will be a rest from major inventions found every year. Man will always be bad as well as good.

OLIVER NAGLE, AGED 11

Exploring

Hundreds of years ago Francis Drake
Explored the seas and found
Quite a few islands, gold and silver.
Thought there were weird green monsters
 in the sea.
He also thought there were ghosts in the rigging,
But that was in the 16th century.

Now in this Millennium,
Which is the space age,
We are going out to explore
The Universe, finding different planets,
Landing on the Moon
And places like that.

When we go to explore
The Universe
In the next Millennium, we would see
Mars, Saturn and Uranus,
Before we land back on Earth again
To our green plants.

TOM SEAL, AGED 9

Dear Children In The Future

I like spellings, topic, diary and maths. I am not so keen on PE and English. At play time I play bulldog with my friends. It's a good game and I like playing chase with the girls. In the summer we go on the grass. I like reading, too. In the future, can you still see out of windows? Have you got your own computer? Do you stand up in assembly? Does the building look old? Have you still got a boat, a bus and a house in the playground? Well, I saw them being made. Does your mum have her own parking spot? Do you still have blackboards? Do you watch television?

ANDREW BENNETT, AGED 7

In the New Millennium I hope that we still have a field to play on.

IMOGEN SMITH, AGED 6

LANGLEY PARK SCHOOL FOR GIRLS

MILLENNIUM MUSES

The countdown's begun for the new century
  to dawn,
People are planning for the first child to be born.
Everyone waits with anticipation it seems,
Let's hope the Millennium can fulfil all
  our dreams.

Few could have predicted events of the last,
As we welcome the new, we remember the past.
Everyone can recall a momentous occasion,
Maybe with sadness, grief, joy and elation.
From man on the moon to Mandela being freed,
The assassination of Kennedy, Princess Di killed
  at speed,
The Berlin Wall coming down, Communism
  did fall,
I could go on forever if I were to mention them all.

Medicine progressed; test-tube babies were born,
Nuclear weapons produced, people's views were
  quite torn.
Technology advanced beyond one's greatest
  thoughts,
Mobile phones and computers were
  easily bought.
As the century changes, our imaginations run wild,
Whether it be adult, teenager, or even a child.
We all have our views on what the future
  will hold,
None of us knows how it will begin to unfold.

Will there be spaceships instead of our cars?
Will there be holidays to Venus or Mars?
Will there be cloning so life never ends?
Will on transplants from animals our
  survival depend?
Will global warming cause us all to burn?
Will brain microchips replace having to learn?
Will euthanasia become the right thing?
We can all only wonder what the Millennium
  will bring.

CARLENE WILLIS, AGED 14

DAEDALUS AND ICARUS REVISITED

Behold! I begin. I tell the tale,
Of angel wings and forgotten dreams,
Of fearless races and cars that gleam,
I refer to the tale of Daedalus and Icarus,
  who met a terrible fate,
But my real tale comes of late,
In as modern a world as can be wished,
Of gang rumbles, fights with guns and fists,
They proposed a race to determine the better,
Across ravaged lands, strangling daises with
  cruel heather,
The headlights burned brightly as the cars
  revved up,
The emotions tore to the point of insanity,
They didn't care who won,
All they wanted was to defy the Sun,
The Sun who trapped them in meaningless lives,

Like Daedalus and Icarus trapped in the labyrinth,
Desperate to be free,
As Daedalus crafted his wings with skill,
The well manicured cars zoomed in for the kill,
And free at last were Daedalus and Icarus,
The gangs in cars,
Beyond boundaries, fences and bars,
But did that ecstasy lead them beyond sense?,
One car flashed past over the fence, over the cliff,
Icarus flew to the Sun,
That was the end of their fun,
They fell like rocks to the sure ocean,
And there was stillness now, after all the
  displaced motion,
All false hopes scattered into the sea,
No time to flee.

HELEN BAKER, AGED 14

21ST CENTURY
AN EXTRACT

*What do you do in school? Do you have
virtual teachers and only use computers for work,
never pen and paper? You don't take notes; you use
dictaphones and you have lessons like genetic
engineering and artificial intelligence
instead of English and Maths.*

ALICE GIBBONS, AGED 13

SILENT THOUGHTS
AN EXTRACT

I'd like to be living
In a place where peace would last,
Where murderers and bloody wars
Are a thing of the past.

I hope when I come to read this
All my dreams have come true,
And all the generations thereafter
Will have peace and harmony too.

SHARLENE HATTON, AGED 15

LITTLE RED RIDING HOOD – 2050
AN EXTRACT

*The year 2050 – four years after the Nuclear
Holocaust. The Earth was now a vast wasteland,
barren and ruined, with scattered settlements
of survivors.*

  *In a deep valley below, a pile of shrapnel which
seemed to reach the sky was what some might
call a small "village", consisting of five small
homemade shacks, which were made of anything
and everything. Noxious gases filled the air.
In one of these little huts lived a woman and*

*her daughter, Little Red Riding Hood but people
called her Lrrh.*

  *One orange-skyed afternoon Lrrh set out to her
grandmother's shack which stood beyond a big,
green marsh. Luckily someone had built a bridge
across the marsh. She hadn't really favoured the
idea of jumping from log to log across the marsh,
not knowing what mutation could reach out from
the green-brown sludge ...*

WENDY SPEAR, AGED 14

STEPHEN PENEYCAD

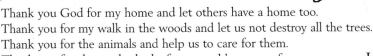

THANK YOU

Thank you God for my home and let others have a home too.
Thank you for my walk in the woods and let us not destroy all the trees.
Thank you for the animals and help us to care for them.
Thank you for those who look after us and keep us safe,
    we want everyone to feel safe and to be kind to each other.
Please stop the bad people fighting.
We want our world to be a happy place full of sunshine.
Please watch over us and help us to think about what we are doing.
Amen.

RECEPTION CLASS, AGED 4–5

DEAR GOD

In the next Millennium, please stop
people fighting each other.
Amen.

MELISSA SEABROOK, AGED 6

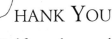

Dear God I wish everyone was friends
Amen

CHARLEY FISHLOCK, AGED 6

THE FARMER AND HIS CHICKENS
A MODERN FABLE

ONE WARM SUNNY AFTERNOON on the farm, the farmer was locking up his buildings ready to go inside to his farmhouse. He stopped by the chicken house to put a bolt across the door.

His chickens were prize chickens and every day that week, one had been killed. Fortunately, his biggest and most magnificent chicken had not been killed. After he had securely locked the chicken house up, he went indoors to have his tea. Later, he would go early to bed because he had to be up early in the morning to look after his animals.

Later, in the night, when it was pitch black, a wolf walked slowly and cautiously towards the chicken house. He sniffed at it and then went round the back to look for the hole he had dug a couple of days ago. He found it and squeezed through the small hole. After squeaks and howls, he caught one of the remaining chickens. He ate it quickly and rushed out of the chicken shed as fast as he could go.

The next day the farmer went out to feed his chickens and found that there were only two left. Not only that, but the wolf had taken his biggest and prize-winning chicken. The farmer was furious. Then he had a wonderful, clever idea. He went to the local store and bought a bottle of deadly wolf poison. He followed the wolf's tracks back to the tree where the wolf lived and emptied the whole bottle out!

That night the wolf didn't go out hunting because he was still full from the night before. He didn't go out but, in the night, it rained. It rained very heavily all night. The deadly wolf poison was washed away from the hole and down towards a nearby river. The poison got washed into the river and into the farmer's water system.

During the night, the farmer's son went downstairs to get a drink of water. He turned on the tap, but the water that flowed out of it was chalk-white and full of poison. The farmer's son couldn't see it because it was so dark.

The next day when the farmer went to get his breakfast, he saw his son lying on the floor. The farmer saw the glass in his hand and knew immediately what had happened. The farmer ran away and never returned.

Moral: Think about how your actions may have an effect on the future.

EMILY FOX, AGED 10

CRIME

It's too fast.
Are we too slow?
Crime is a tower of strength,
But justice is a small weak flat.

We need justice.
So give Britain its great name back.
And make the whole world a better
*   place to live in,*
For the Millennium.

BOBBY SIMPSON, AGED 11

In the Millennium I wish that people in
other countries had enough food.

KERRIANNE COOPER, AGED 6

MILLENNIUM SONG

The new Millennium is near
Get the message, loud and clear.
For all the children we want to see
A fulfilling future, for you and me.

No more crying, no more trouble
Start right now, at the double.

We have a dream we'd like to share
Of happiness, love and care
We'd like to tell it to the nation
During the Millennium celebration.

No more crying, no more trouble
Start right now, at the double.

We want to see an end to war
To share our money among the poor
Building loving, caring homes
So let's hope we're not alone.

No more crying, no more trouble
Start right now, at the double.

Some people do not care
Their attitude isn't fair!
They can be selfish and be greedy
We must work together, to help the needy.

No more crying, no more trouble
Start right now, at the double.

CLASS T, AGED 10–11

ILLUSTRATIONS BY CLASS G, AGED 6–7

MANOR OAK PRIMARY SCHOOL

FREDDIE'S WISH

My wish is that all the people from Kosovo get a home so they can live in peace and have healthier lives. I wish football players could come to my house. I wish I played for Arsenal.

FREDDIE REEVES, AGED 10

GENTY'S WISH

I wish that my nan and all the good people came alive because I love her lots.

GENTY LEE, AGED 7

DAVE'S WISH

I wish I had a motorbike
I wish I was 36
I wish I was a football player
I wish I won a World Cup
I wish I could ride a horse
I wish I could drive a car
I wish I had a motorbike

DAVE VINCENT, AGED 8

MOSES' WISH

I wish people would stop chopping down trees. We need them to live. Stop killing birds by putting chemicals on the grass. I want the world to be a place where people and animals live in peace.

MOSES DEVALL, AGED 7

Mums and dads stop child abuse
Illnesses and diseases to be cured
Like everyone and get along
Like each other for who they are
Everyone has a home
No crimes and murders
No cruelty or unkindness
I wish for people to stop wars
Unhappiness to be banished
Me and you can stop all this

CHRISTOPHER PARKER, AGED 10

LINDA'S DREAM

My wish for the Millenium is to be a musician and other people to become what they want to be. The world should be a better place for everybody, not just for one person. Nobody should be poorer or richer than each other. They need to be all the same. I can't promise anything but I wish everybody has a good life before they pass away.

LINDA NTUMY, AGED 11

MILLENNIUM

We want peace.
No cutting down rainforests.
No robbing banks.
Be kind to everyone.

JOHN SCHOCK, AGED 9x

WHAT LUKE WANTS

Things I want for my Millennium ...
I hope more things will be recycled, rather than chucking rubbish away.

A list of things to recycle:
Cans, bottles, paper, plastic, sweet wrappers, crisp packets, and garden rubbish.

LUKE WILLIAMS, AGED 7

Pray for peace around the world
Equal rights
All be kind
Co-operate
Everyone likes peace.

LUKE STRONG, AGED 10

SAVE THE ANIMALS

I wish the animals would stay alive. We must stop cutting down trees and bushes. They must have homes to live in. We can help them continue in the land and be safe by feeding them and helping them. It is good to have animals in the land.

RACHEL LEE, AGED 7

The Angry Pixie

ONE DAY THERE WAS A PIXIE called Inkey and she always wore a pink coat. At 12 o'clock she went to a fair and went on some rides and got some pink and yellow sweets.

Just as she was going to another ride she saw her friend, who was a fairy. "Hello," she said. They went on the roundabout together and when they got off a gnome came and started bullying her. She started to cry. The fairy put a spell on him and the gnome fell asleep and lay down on the floor until morning.

In the morning Inkey got up and went to the shops. She had forgotten about the gnome bullying her. The gnome was in the shop. The gnome tried to say sorry but the fairy and the pixie said: "No! We don't like you any more."

Moral: Think before you act.

ROSIE CHRISTY AND CHELSEA CURTIS, AGED 10

The Good Path

The Naughty Path

Millennium Wishes

I wish that all the bad things will go and all the good things will stay.

MATTHEW SHIRLEY, AGED 7

My wish for the Millennium is to stop the bad things, and to make a happy world.

BETH O'REGAN, AGED 7

Tom And The Ugly Brothers
A Modern Fairy Tale

ONCE UPON A TIME there lived two very ugly brothers and a boy called Tom. They lived in a little wooden hut.

Tom was the slave around the house, he wasn't allowed to do anything apart from work. The two ugly brothers were called Matthew and Ben and they were covered in warts and spots.

One day they announced, "We're going to the local disco so, ha, ha, ha, ha," and out of their pockets came the disco passes and out of Matthew's pocket a third pass fluttered to the floor. "Oh goody," exclaimed Tom, "I can go too." Matthew quickly picked it up before Tom could move and tore it up into tiny squares and off he and Ben skipped chanting, "We're going to a disco." Tom looked sadly at the grubby wooden floor and carried on scrubbing.

That night when Matthew and Ben had gone to the disco, a robot teleported to Tom's house and said, "You may go to the disco."

"But I haven't got a hall pass," protested Tom.

"Well you have now," and with that the robot waved his magic spanner and in Tom's hand a hall pass appeared.

"What am I going to wear?" asked Tom.

"Well, go and get me two screws and an oil can." The robot waved his magic spanner again and the oil can turned into a motorised skateboard and the screws turned into a designer outfit.

"You can't keep these clothes, and you have to be back by 12 o'clock," and with that Tom jumped on to his high speed skateboard and took off.

At the disco Tom met the most beautiful girl any eyes could be placed on. He found out that her name was Mary and she was the Prime Minister's daughter. Tom walked gingerly up to her and asked for a dance. To Tom's surprise, she said, "Yes."

Suddenly, the clock struck twelve, "Oh no, I have to run," said Tom and with that he took off. On his way out his Nike shoe fell off without him noticing and he ran all the way home.

The next week the Prime Minister's daughter sent out all her guard robots for people to try on the shoe, and whoever it fitted she would marry. When the robot got to Tom's house, Tom thought that it looked like his trainer. When he tried it on he said, "It fits."

A cheer went up. He got taken to Mary and they got married straight away. They lived happily ever after.

SIMON SPIER, AGED 11

WISHES AND THOUGHTS

I wish that people like me could walk in the future.

I wish that people will always have family and friends.

I hope that all crime will go.

I hope to stay in bed all day long!

I wish people would stop killing animals.

I wish that the bombing and all that stuff would stop.

I hope all wild animals are protected so they don't get killed.

CHARLI, THOMAS, DAVID, SIMON, AMY, NICKI AND HOLLY, CLASS G2A, AGED 10–11

THINGS WE LOVE AND HATE

Thank you for helping me to care for my baby birds so that they survived. Their future is now safe.

Thank you for my grandma – she died in August, and I'll always remember her.

I wish that the war now going on would stop.

Thank you for my new cat. My old cat died and I miss it. I will give this cat a good future.

I want Kosovo to end and the war to stop.

Thank you for taking my pony called Toffee to a retirement home because he's old. My best friend took him in his horsebox. He will have a good future.

PATRICK, ADAM, STACEY, HANNAH, LUCY, RUPERT, DAVID, BARRY, SAM, JENNIFER AND PAUL, CLASS G3A, AGED 12–13

THOUGHTS FOR THE FUTURE

To let everyone be treated as equals and have the same opportunities in life, whatever needs they have.

THE COOPERS GROUP, AGED 11–16 '98–'99

HOPE

We hope for peace and for fair shares around the world.

MARK, MATTHEW, POLLY, FRANK, MICHAEL, JODIE, FRANKIE AND DANIELLA, CLASS G3B, AGED 11–12

WISHES AND HOPES

I wish the sun was out every day.
I wish I were strong.
I hope mum's baby comes soon.
I hope there are no more wars.
I wish I was going out with my dad.
We all hope that we have things to enjoy at home and at school.

DANNY, FOZIA, DAVID, CRAIG, PAUL, CHRISTIAN, LILLY AND SIMON, CLASS G2B, AGED 7–9

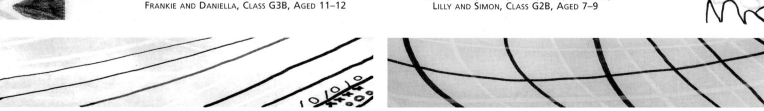

MEAD ROAD INFANT SCHOOL

I want big brothers and sisters to
be kind to each other.

MEGAN PHILLIPS, AGED 5

I want everyone
to be good to each other.

BEN POOLEY, AGED 5

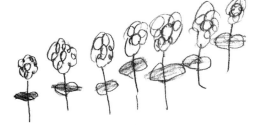

I would like lots of flowers
growing everywhere.

MADELEINE BATE, AGED 4

I want to see lots of trees.

JOE HOLSGROVE, AGED 5

Keep the world clean and the world tidy. Stop using guns.

ALEX BALL, AGED 7

I don't want too many soldiers, because
there is too much fighting.

ELLIOT GORDON, AGED 5

I want lots of fields full of buttercups
Jordy woodhead

JORDY WOODHEAD, AGED 5

"Small enough for everyone to count."

I want people to be good to each other. No arguing.

JAMES RAWLINGS, AGED 5

I don't want anyone to spoil the world.

HARRY BRAYBROOKE, AGED 6

To hope people don't get hurt. To have no houses in
the countryside. So rich people give poor people
some of their money.

JAMES ANDERSON, AGED 6

I hope there isn't any wars.

TOMMY ROWE, AGED 6

PEACE FOR A DAY

IN THE NEW MILLENNIUM I think that schools and colleges will celebrate worldwide and charities will increase donations for the homeless. That day schools will probably have no school just for that day.

People will, at least I think they will, make a new Millennium resolution and I think the council will as well. And I think that Kosovo will stop fighting for one day, like England and Germany on Christmas Day. I hope more Special Needs Schools will be in the borough and I hope this school, The Meadow, doesn't close down.

One hundred years from now things are going to be different. TV is going to have more channels. Peace will come to some countries and war to others, and other things will be out of fashion. Different sports will come in and out of fashion. The council will be different, hopefully better, but crime will increase. More police will come, at least I hope so.

Designer labels will fade away and new ones will come. At least I think so, because this is 1999, not 2099.

CHRISTIAN THOMPSON, AGED 12

ALL CHANGE

I think that the year 2000 will be a time to remember. The Millennium Dome is opening and the National Maritime Museum will have another 12 brand new galleries and the new Jubilee Line extension will run between London Charing Cross and Stratford.

It will be a wonderful time for everybody with millions of people watching a party on television and a street party will begin and there will be fireworks at the River Thames at Greenwich.

There will be new rules and new laws and we will have a lovely new mayor for London. We may have Olympics in Sydney in Australia.

ANDREW BLANDFORD, AGED 12

BE GOOD TO NATURE

THE NEW WORLD IS NOT the new world, it is the same world with pollution in it. There are bricks to make houses but all it's doing is killing us so, cut down the pollution and maybe we can live in houses but not too many, so don't go over the limit.

No more cutting trees down, maybe we need paper but think about the air and especially the ozone layer because it's over the limit and killing all of nature's creatures and creatures are scared of us. So stop killing creatures and people, stop chopping trees down, stop making guns and tanks and mines on the ground, or Mother Nature will strike back and make havoc and burn us out of this world.

So don't go over the limit or nature will go over the limit and when nature goes over the limit you don't want to get in its way.

So don't go over the line and especially don't forget the things that are in this world because you are in the world too. So don't ruin history and don't go over the line.

KERRY HOLGATE, AGED 13

PARTY TIME!

I think there will be lots of parties everywhere and the street will be packed and the cabs will be full. I hope I can go to a party with my dad. I think Chris will still be my best friend.

JAMES STEVENS, AGED 13

Midfield Primary School

Eleanor's Promise

I will help people that are in danger.
I will put my rubbish in the bin.
I will be good and kind.
I will help the animals.
I will look after people.

ELEANOR BANKS, AGED 7

A Prayer Of Hope

Sunshine,
Rainfall,
Trees grow,
Flowers bloom,
Children play,
People eat,
Rivers flow,
Wars end,
FOREVER.
Amen.

JOHN BUGLER, AGED 12

Tom And Jerry

Tom was playing football.
He was good at it, Jerry wasn't.
Tom said, "I'm good at it" and
didn't keep trying. But Jerry
is going to practise. So Jerry
got in the football team.
He played for Mousechester.
**Moral: Keep trying and
you will succeed.**

SEAN HILLIAR, AGED 6

Lucy Lion And Zara Zebra

Lucy was a lion. Every day she
chased a zebra called Zara. One
day Lucy was chasing Zara. Lucy
tripped over a stone and hurt her
leg. Zara helped Lucy on to her
feet. After that Lucy the Lion
never chased a zebra again.

**Moral: Be nice to others and
they will be nice to you.**

JERRY MURRELL, AGED 9

Victoria's Hope

My hope for the future is
that people who are nasty
start being nice because
then everyone will
have lots of
friends.

VICTORIA GRAYSTONE,
AGED 8

George's Wish

*I wish that people would always
say please and thank you.*

GEORGE SHOTTLE, AGED 5

A Poem For The Millennium

In the year 2000
   it is the Millennium,
They are the words
   to jump out and say.
There is a building
   for the Millennium.
I hope it will be great
   in the Millennium,
And I hope
   in the year 2000,
Everybody will have homes,
   so that they are happy.
There'll be different money,
   there'll be different things,
We'll have a new start,
   we'll be jumping for joy,
We'll all be working as hard
   as can be.
It will be great,
   in the Millennium.

AMY JOLLIFFE, AGED 9

Reece's Hope

I hope that everybody is happy.
I hope that the world is safe.

REECE CHURCHER, AGED 6

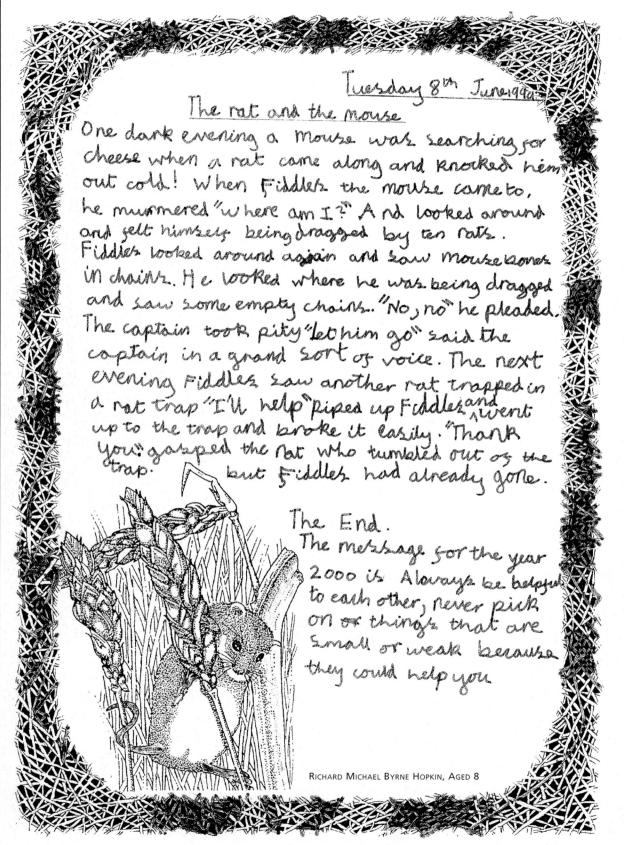

Tuesday 8ᵗʰ June 1999

The rat and the mouse

One dark evening a mouse was searching for cheese when a rat came along and knocked him out cold! When Fiddles the mouse came to, he murmered "where am I?" And looked around and felt himself being dragged by ten rats. Fiddles looked around again and saw mouse bones in chains. He looked where he was being dragged and saw some empty chains. "No, no" he pleaded. The captain took pity "let him go" said the captain in a grand sort of voice. The next evening Fiddles saw another rat trapped in a rat trap "I'll help" piped up Fiddles and went up to the trap and broke it easily. "Thank you" gasped the rat who tumbled out of the trap. but Fiddles had already gone.

The End.
The message for the year 2000 is Always be helpful to each other, never pick on or things that are small or weak because they could help you

RICHARD MICHAEL BYRNE HOPKIN, AGED 8

MY WISH FOR THE FUTURE

I wish that there would be no more disasters like floods, tornadoes and bombings because lots of people die, even little children. I think we should try harder to keep the environment clean so plants and animals can live better. We should have respect for all animals and build safaris for animals to live in the wild instead of being kept in cages because they are sad in zoos and miss the other animals.

MATTHEW GIBNEY, AGED 7

I hope people keep our world clean.
LAUREN N

I want everybody to be happy.
KAYLEIGH

I wish that everybody had toys
MAX

I hope nobody kicks somebody.
KIRSTY

I hope that people don't fight otherwise people get hurt.
SHAQUILLE

people should be tidy.
DILLON

I think that we should help people who are deaf.
COURTNEY

I To hope that live people on don't the have streets.
ALICE

I wish that the world was safe.
SAINA

I wish that everybody would be friendly.
SHAIMA

I think people should listen to other people.
GRACE

I wish that all people could read and write.
JAMES

I wish that people wouldnot kill animals.
ALEXANDER

I think blind people should have guide dogs.
I think people should not interrupt
I think people should not kick
NIKHIL

I hope that robbers wouldn't rob old people.
TRISTAN

I would like to help children because they have no equipment
JOSHUA

people shouldn't push other people and other people shouldn't push them back.
LAUREN M

when people fall down the stairs you will have to help them up.
THOMAS

I wish that everybody was kind.
COURTNEY

I wish that everybody will have water.
THOMAS G

SARAH MEAD, AGED 14

A FABLE OF NOTHING

ONCE UPON A TIME, there was a Creator. The Creator was a peaceful being and enjoyed His own company. (We will assume He is male but, as you will later find out, genders had not yet been created). He was happy, just alone with His own thoughts, not sharing His existence. It was for this reason that He created Nothing. He did not create light, not even dark, only Nothing. There was not even an empty space, there was Nothing.

This Nothing that the Creator made instilled in Him a deep peace, and He felt amazingly satisfied. This satisfaction stayed with Him for a long time. (One would probably assume millions of years, but time had not yet been created). Unfortunately, after a while, an unease started growing inside Him. He became bored and restless and was unhappy because He could not boast about the wonderful, peaceful Nothing He had made. So the Creator created Ado.

The Creator said to Ado, "Look at this wonderful Nothing I have made! Rejoice with me and make Ado."

And this is what Ado did. He had parties, for which the Creator had to create People, to celebrate Nothing. Once there were People, Nature had to be created to support People and, as Time evolved, the World as we know it had been created and Nothing was lost forever.

The Creator became sad because He would never have the wonderful calm of Nothing again. He only had much Ado.

Moral: Don't make much ado about nothing.

TO THE PEOPLE OF THE FUTURE

In the future will we find life on other planets?

In the future will we be living on the Moon?

In the future will we explore another galaxy?

In the future will people live forever
and call getting old an illness?

In the future will people
forget the past?

What will we come to?

Save the Aliens

A WISH

1999 *I wish for world peace.*
2000 *Has world peace come yet?*
2100 *Yet?*
2500 *Now?*
2750 *Has it happened yet?*
3000 *?*
...?
When?

CLASS 7SZ, AGED 11

Oak Lodge Primary School

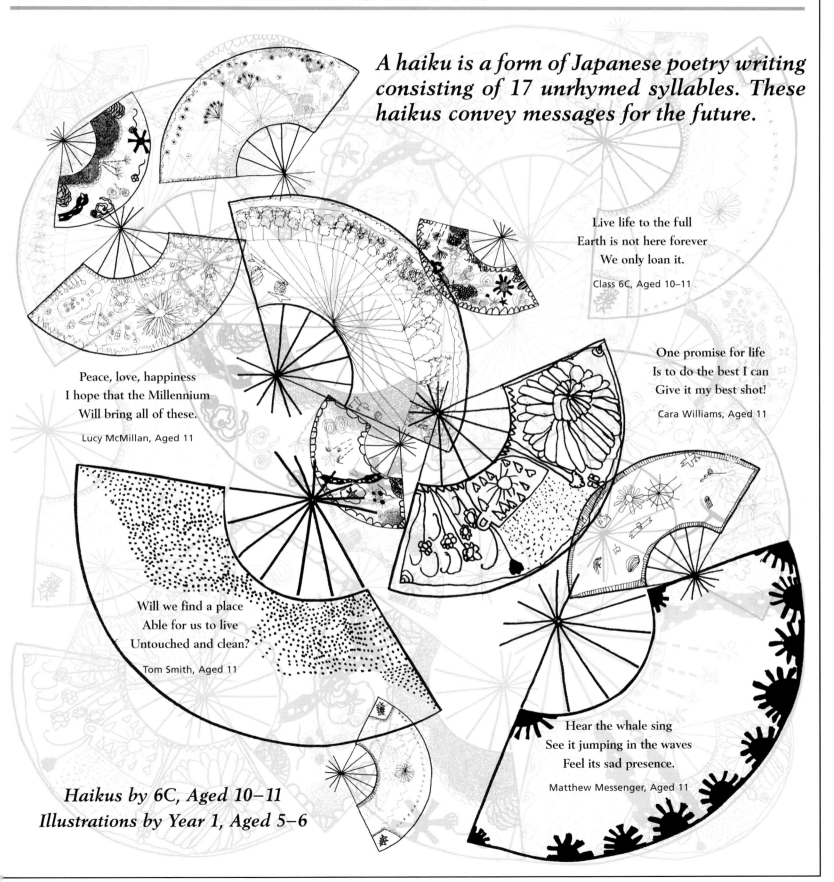

A haiku is a form of Japanese poetry writing consisting of 17 unrhymed syllables. These haikus convey messages for the future.

Live life to the full
Earth is not here forever
We only loan it.

Class 6C, Aged 10–11

One promise for life
Is to do the best I can
Give it my best shot!

Cara Williams, Aged 11

Peace, love, happiness
I hope that the Millennium
Will bring all of these.

Lucy McMillan, Aged 11

Will we find a place
Able for us to live
Untouched and clean?

Tom Smith, Aged 11

Hear the whale sing
See it jumping in the waves
Feel its sad presence.

Matthew Messenger, Aged 11

Haikus by 6C, Aged 10–11
Illustrations by Year 1, Aged 5–6

Emma went into the funfair,
and what did Emma feel?
Emma felt a long soft elephant's trunk
eating orange peel.

EMMA BONE, AGED 7

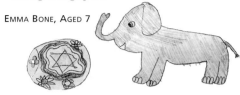

Shemaine went down to the jungle,
and what did Shemaine see?
Shemaine saw a crocodile
looking for its tea.

SARAH WILDBORE, AGED 7

Becky went into the village,
and what did Becky hear?
Becky heard a screeching cat
very very near.

REBECCA THOMSON, AGED 7

Scott went into the airfair,
and what did Scott hear?
Scott heard an army aeroplane,
it came near and near and near.

SCOTT KENT, AGED 7

Emma went into the future,
and what did Emma hear?
Emma heard babies talking
very very clear.

Mum

Dad

Hello

EMMA BONE, AGED 7

Poem

I am the wing on a lovely butterfly.
I am the lovely butterfly flying in the air.
I am the air blowing the tree.
I am the tree with the ant.
I am the ant on the colourful leaf.
I am the leaf falling to the ground.
I am the ground with people running.
I am the people on the playground.
I am the playground with the toys.
I am the toys being used.

NIKKITA PAMMENT, AGED 7

Joshua went into the future,
and what did Joshua see?
Joshua saw a chimpanzee
swinging on a tree.

JOSHUA STIMSON, AGED 7

Rosemary went into the future,
and this is what Rosemary saw.
Rosemary saw a spaceship
dancing on the floor.

ROSEMARY HORSLEY, AGED 7

Joshua went into the big wood,
and what did Joshua see?
Joshua saw an animal
eating a juicy pea.

JOSHUA FIELD, AGED 7

Melissa went into the future,
and what did Melissa see?
Melissa saw people talking on the video phone.
That seems very strange to me.

MELISSA CASE, AGED 7

Sophie went into the jungle,
and what did Sophie see?
Sophie saw a big bad tiger,
and it tried to eat me!

SOPHIE HAGGAR, AGED 7

Jake went into the future, and what did Jake see?
Jake saw a dinosaur playing with some bees.

JAKE STEPHENS, AGED 7

Jake went into the airfair, and what did Jake see?
Jake saw some Red Arrows acrobating before tea.

JAKE STEPHENS, AGED 7

Debbie went into the future,
and what did Debbie find?
She found a robot instead of a teacher,
but she didn't really mind.

DEBORAH HOLLAND, AGED 7

I Wonder...

I wonder what would happen
If all the tigers died,
And the elephants and rhinos,
Would any wildlife survive?

I wonder what would happen
If all the forests were chopped down,
Would we gasp for breath and die
Or would we still live on?

I wonder what will happen
If pollution filled the Earth,
Would all plants and creatures die?
Will we see a cleaner sky?

In my new future world
Wild animals won't be hunted,
They won't become extinct,
And forests will not be destroyed.

I wonder what will happen
In the new Millennium?

Year 4, Aged 8–9
From an idea by Matthew Weeks, Aged 9

The Millennium Bug

I've just seen a Millennium bug,
They're tiny, pink and blue.
One wrecked the whole of my computer,
One might wreck yours too.

Just because of the Millennium digits,
This Millennium bug went mad!
Tore up the whole of my computer
(horrible, selfish, little lad!).

So watch out for Millennium bugs,
They're tiny, pink and blue,
One wrecked the whole of my computer,
Mind – or one might wreck yours too!

Holly Gaston, Aged 11

Mark McCarthy, Aged 10

My Millennium Prayer

Dear God,
I hope that all the wars will stop!
I hope that hovercrafts and cars will be
battery powered and not petrol or diesel,
so that will cause less pollution.
Amen.

Matthew Eastwood, Aged 8

2001

Wouldn't it be fun,
In the year 2001?
The cars will fly,
The robots will clean,
And put your clothes
In the washing machine.

Grace Smithen, Aged 8

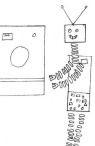

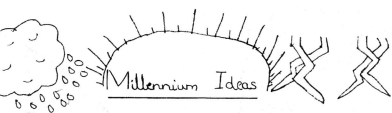

In the Millennium I would hope for a better weather system, so if we were to have a storm it could get us ready and prepared for what might happen!

Charlotte Singleton and Kate Bowyer,
Aged 10

Dear God

In the Millennium let there be no wars in other countries such as Kosovo.

In the Millennium let there be peace.

In the Millennium let there be more doctors and no more sicknesses.

Amen.

Laura Sutton, Aged 8

Work as a team • Be kind • Put others first • Think about the environment • Love your neighbours •

Money isn't everything • Respect other people • Listen to your conscience • Don't boast • Don't fight

THE REFUGEE

The pain was unbearable having to say goodbye to another world, to leave another family. Tears blurred her vision and stuck to the hair covering her eyes, making it glisten like a ruby.

Today the gender war had broken out, that meant that females visiting Mars and males visiting Venus had to leave. She remembered the day she had left Venus, she remembered the slight headache she'd had after her real name had been erased from her memory and she remembered her pride at being renamed Pilgrim 2946. That headache had felt like a breeze compared to the tempest thrashing inside her head now.

She focused on the present again and ran to pack up all her belongings into her bag and then went to the holo-projector. It confirmed her worst fears, every female on Mars would be destroyed unless they arrived at Shuttle Board 1 in 15 minutes!

Shuttle Board 1 was in the centre of the city and 2946 was at the outskirts of it. There were about 20 minutes between them, 20 minutes she didn't have. She flung herself at the door and started running, she did not look back until she was halfway there.

When she arrived at the shuttles she was sweating hard, her plain brown robe and her red hair stuck to her like skin. She quickly joined the queue. She was near the end of the line and when she checked her chronometer she only had a few minutes left. As she found

her seat, the alarm went off meaning the guards (all males – BIG surprise) could shoot, but she was safe now. The laser shots bounced harmlessly off the ship's sides. Once in space the captain gave the bad news they would not be allowed to return to Venus. It turned out they, and the returning males, would be transported to a strange planet called Earth.

What would Earth hold? 2946 did not know!

SAM GRAYSTON, AGED 11

THE MOUSE AND THE CAT

One fine, spring day a cat called Kitty went to visit her best friend Corney the mouse. They played all day in the sun. Finally the sun set and Kitty said, "Hey, Corney, wear these tomorrow!" and with that she threw him a bottle of pretend cat fur. The next day Corney was all dressed up like a cat. (Kitty was not there because she was ill.) Corney went out to find his friend Cheese. When he found him Cheese ran away in fright. So all day Corney sat alone. At night time Corney's mum nearly fainted but still she knew it was Corney. She brought him in and wiped all the fur off and said, "Don't let Kitty do that again!" and he didn't do it again. The next day Kitty came to Corney's house to play. Corney said, "Kitty please don't change me again. It was awful." "OK," replied Kitty and she never did.

Moral: Everyone is unique – your friends shouldn't try to change you.

ALEXANDRA NEWMAN, AGED 8

• Think of others • Plan things before you do them • Don't judge people by their appearance •

Perry Hall Primary School

How The Frog Became

ONE FINE DAY God was in His garden pulling out all of the weeds when all of a sudden a little pear shaped bean popped out of the ground and grew round in just a matter of seconds. God went inside to look at a flower dictionary but just couldn't find the matching seed.

God spent some time with the bean to have a good look at it. It was gradually getting smaller and smaller by the hour so He waited until the next day to finish His work and spend some time to investigate the unusual bean.

The next day God went out to finish His work without noticing the bean that He was growing. He was just about to start work when He saw a little black dot wriggling beside a sphere that was almost see-through.

God was shocked. He did not have a clue how this little bean could have formed into a creature in just a matter of days. The creature was just a little bit like a two-legged creature. God was thinking about giving the creature a name and after a while, because it was so obvious, He said "I've got it!"

God called the creature a tadpole for 12 days until the tadpole grew two front legs and its tail grew shorter. The tadpole was now jumping to and fro in God's garden and it began to make a croak instead of a squeak noise. God kept it in for the night to cure the croak but it did not work.

God did not think that tadpole was the right name for a creature that can jump, so he called it a frog to say it jumps to and FRO in God's garden, which spells FROG. God soon let the frog go but the croak was never cured. That is how the Frog became.

JAMES GRAHAM, AGED 10

Bringing The Rain To Kapiti Plain

Once upon a time there was a great big plain.

It was called Kapiti Plain. Kapiti Pain had an ocean of green grass. Kapiti Plain always rained. There were loads of trees for the giraffes.

But! One day the rain was so very belated. The animals migrated. The cows got dry, hungry and skinny. Ki-pat was so small he didn't know what to do. The ocean of nice green grass turned to crunchy brown dead grass.

The cows suffered from so much sun and no rain. Just then a big black cloud shifted its way over to Kapiti Plain. It made a big dark grey shadow on Kapiti Plain.

Ki-pat said to himself, "This might give a bit of luck." The cows mooed for the big black cloud. The giraffes stretched their necks as high as they could. But they just couldn't reach the cloud.

Ki-pat was so worried. But then an eagle fluttered by. The eagle dropped a feather that helped to change the weather. Ki-pat took the feather and he made an arrow with it and a slender stick.

He shot it and it popped the cloud – it started to rain. All the animals came back.

Ki-pat got married and had a son.

KRISTI CORMACK, AGED 7

The Fox And The Chicken

ONE DAY A GRUMPY FARMER had one lazy chicken. The chicken was called Dopy and the farmer was called Trevor.

One day the fat farmer said "Dopy get up, you lazybones."

"Yes Trevor, and stop being bossy."

"I'm bossy because you woke me up at 5 o'clock in the morning" said the tired farmer. "Anyway, here's your food."

The lazy chicken ate his food like a greedy chicken. As he was eating his dinner a sly fox passed by and said "Come here and you can have some more food, it's just the same. If you eat it, it will make you strong."

He thought "mmmmmmmm!" So he went through the hole in the fence but he was too fat so the clever fox said as he ate, "That teaches you not to believe everything you hear."

Want Some Food ?

At 5 o'clock, the brainy farmer said "Dopy, where are you?" but there was nothing there. The next day the farmer went out looking for him but he couldn't find him anywhere. So the very sad farmer started to cry. "Waaaaaaaaaa!"

The very next day the excited farmer went to the pet shop and bought a plastic toy chicken and called it Happy. "Well it's better than no chickens at all!" he laughed.

Moral: Never listen to other people that sound sly.

TANYA SANDERSON, AGED 9

Pickhurst Infant School

How To Make The World A Better Place In The New Millennium

Make the world more beautiful with roses books and trees.

Make cakes

Build houses so everyone has a home.

CLASS RB, AGED 5

A Millennium Fable

There was a frog by a pond with his wife on the edge of the pond. Then a cat came out of the house and saw the frogs on the edge of the pond. The frogs didn't see the cat because they were facing the other side of the pond. The cat went up close to the frogs and then the frogs turned round and said, "What can I do for you?"
"Oh nothing," said the cat to the frogs. But he really did want something. He wanted to eat them all up in one gulp. But he didn't because he had talked to the frogs.
Moral: Talk to each other.

MATHEW SWANNACK, AGED 7

Our Millennium Wish

We wish that we could plant lots of trees
  and flowers.
We wish that people would not chop down trees.
We wish that everywhere could be pretty
  and tidy.
We wish we could tell people not to break
  animals' homes.
We wish that everyone could be kind to animals.
We wish we could tell people not to hurt
  other people.
We wish that we could cheer sad people up.
We wish that we could make everyone happy.

CLASS RJM, AGED 5

In My World I Would Like

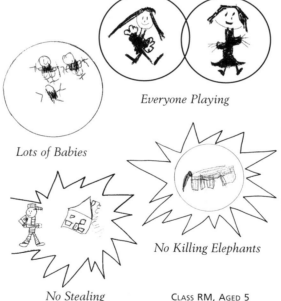

Everyone Playing

Lots of Babies

No Killing Elephants

No Stealing   CLASS RM, AGED 5

Life In 2000

Today in 1999 we go on holiday to the beach or the countryside. In the future we will visit different planets. We will get there by rocket. Aliens will take us to different places.
Today in 1999 we all go to school. We all write on paper and we have a piece each. In the future we will all have computers.

ALICE SYMONDS, AGED 7

In The Year 2000

We would like to be kind to people,
We would like to be kind to each other,
We would like to play fair games,
We would like to be kind to animals,
We would like to look after our cats,
We would like the world to be a happy place!

CLASS RP, AGED 5

The Rubbish Eater
WILLIAM WILKES-HAWKINS, AGED 6

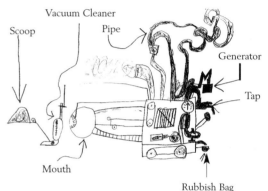

Scoop · Vacuum Cleaner · Pipe · Generator · Tap · Mouth · Rubbish Bag

The House Of Tomorrow

My house has a code to get in and robbers can't get in. I have an electric table that moves where you want it. There is a chair that moves out of the wall. We have a robot that cleans up for you. I have a water-bed that you can sleep on. I have a TV which you can order things from. The robot washes up for you and he gets the food. When it gets dark, glow-in-the-dark lights come for you and when you want to go to bed they go out for you. The house is made of plastic and you can move it where you like it.

LUAY DAHAN, AGED 7

In the new Millennium I would like to be a weatherman and I will make sure the weather will be very good.

JOSHUA HANCOCK, AGED 6

PICKHURST JUNIOR SCHOOL

MY MILLENNIUM HOPES

Make a cake

Yachting

Whale watching

Ice hockey

Sail a boat

Horse ride

Elephant riding

Swimming lessons

AMY DENIS, AGED 7

---

*My thoughts and hopes for the year 2000 would be
I wish the world would live in peace and harmony
Let there be more cures for serious illnesses
Let the world be full of much more happiness
Enjoy life while it's there for you
Never give up, it's something you must do
Now please let's help the people out on the street
It's something Diana tried to complete
Unite everyone, we've been waiting a while
Millennium is here, everyone wear a smile.*

SADIE TAYLOR, AGED 10

OUR FAMILIES

We hope that our families can live in peace,
harmony, and be healthy in the new Millennium.
That all the children in the family behave well,
don't fight with each other and stay
safe and happy. Most important, our wish is
for love, care and security in our families.

YEAR 4, AGED 8–9

THE EARTH

*Wars are terrible hurtful things,
Poverty and homelessness disease brings,
Animals are now becoming extinct,
Starvation is horrifying I think,
Pollution is happening all over the place,
Everywhere on planet Earth's face.
If I had a wish, just one wish,
I would wish that peace would reign,
The ozone layer would be whole again,
That poverty and disease would disappear,
That extinct animals would reappear.*

CATHERINE MACKINTOSH, AGED 10

*I hope that there will be world peace
in the new Millennium*

ROSS McGEOWN, AGED 10

 2000

*It's New Year's Eve year '99
One min 'til the clock does chime
Thirty seconds the clock still tick
I hope for the Millennium
We can help the sick
Twenty seconds more and we could stop war
Ten seconds left and we could throw away debt
Twelve o'clock now and we all have food to eat
So celebrate the happy day
Now everything's ok.*

NICK OLIVER, AGED 11

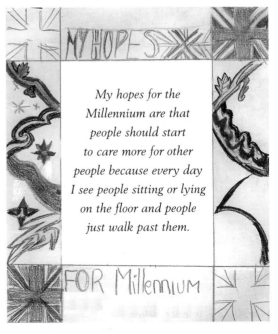

*My hopes for the
Millennium are that
people should start
to care more for other
people because every day
I see people sitting or lying
on the floor and people
just walk past them.*

ROSALIND HAND, AGED 9

my Hopes For Britain in the
millennium

I hope that by the year 2000 they
would have invented some kind of
mashine like a hovering wheel chair,
that would help and would be fun
for disabled people. It would be much
more interesting for them because
they miss out on so much.

GRACE McAULIFFE, AGED 9

I wish there were no burglurs then you could live in peace and no car alarms going off and no house alarms going off.

I wish the car engines were much quieter then you will not have headaces.

by Absolom martin.

age 7 years old.

Short Stories With Morals For The Millennium

WRENS AND KESTRELS CLASS, AGED 5–6

THERE WAS A LITTLE GIRL. She went out without her Mummy telling her to. She went to the shops to get herself a new toy. She saw a stranger, "Oh no!" she said, and she ran back home. "Mummy said I am a naughty girl. I promise I will never do it again."

Moral: Never talk to strangers.

ONE DAY A LITTLE GIRL went to the sweet shop and got lots of sweets and ate them all and she got fat and her teeth fell out and would not grow again.

Moral: Don't eat too many sweets.

Bad Bill

BILL WAS SAD AND LONELY. He had no friends to boss or play with. He thought about his behaviour and how horrible he was to everyone. He decided to be kind and say sorry to his old friends. They all played with Bill and had a great time.

Moral: Be kind to each other.

YEAR 1, AGED 6

ONCE UPON A TIME there was a lazy boy who did not do any work and did not learn at school. But one day, he went to sleep in class and the teacher woke him up. Then he was not lazy again. He learnt lots of different things and was really, really good at school.

Moral: Don't be lazy in school.

ONCE UPON A TIME there was a boy called Charlie and he played too many PlayStation games. So he had square eyes and he didn't learn how to read. He couldn't read people's stories, he was very sad. One day, his PlayStation broke and he was bored and he decided to read his story book.

Moral: Don't play too much PlayStation.

The Spider And The Ant

ONE DAY A SPIDER MET AN ANT. They made friends. One day the spider was trapped, the ant was terrified. The spider was trapped under a stone. The ant tried and tried so hard to lift the stone until he could lift it up. "Thank you, thank you so much," said the spider.

Moral: Always help people when you can, even if you don't know them.

KAYLEIGH OLIVER, AGED 7

The Cat And The Pig

ONCE UPON A TIME there was a pig called Frank. Frank lived on a farm. Lots of other animals lived there too. The farmer and his wife looked after all of their animals and loved them all. The farmer had a cat called Ruby. Ruby did not like Frank. She tried to scratch him, she tried to bite him. She even called him names.

One day it was Frank's Birthday. Frank had a party but he did not invite Ruby. The animals had lots of fun at the party. Ruby was sad and cross because she missed all the fun. Frank went to Ruby and told her why she had not been invited to this party. Ruby learnt that she should be kind and friendly so that people would want to be her friend.

WAGTAILS CLASS, AGED 4–5

Millennium Fable

ONE SPRING DAY IN A FOREST by a tree in a hole, lived a family of foxes. Every night the father goes out hunting with his little boy. Every night they go to a barn of chickens and kill some, but the boy does not get any, so he goes hungry. The next night they went out to hunt but he still came home hungry. Now it was the third night out, so they went to the barn to catch some chickens. He ran after them and caught two and his Dad was proud of him.

Moral: If at first you don't succeed try, try, try again.

SARAH HORNSBY, AGED 10

The Crocodile And The Owl

AN OLD CROCODILE SENT OUT WORD that he was ill and he wanted all the animals and birds to visit him. Most went, but the owl did not. Finally the crocodile sent for him. The owl was asked, "Why did you not come?" The owl replied, "I planned to, but I noticed that many tracks led into your cave, but none came out."

Moral: Don't just follow the crowd.

DARREN SALTER, AGED 10

PRATTS BOTTOM PRIMARY SCHOOL

21ST CENTURY

In the 21st century, in the 21st century,
Don't use cars as much.
In the 21st century, in the 21st century,
Use an alternative mode of transport.
In the 21st century, in the 21st century,
Why don't you think about walking?
In the 21st century, in the 21st century!

AMY COPPOCK, AGED 9

ANNA STOREY,
AGED 7

THE LAST BREADCRUMB

THERE WAS A POOR OLD MAN who lived in a
forest. Often his friend the bird would come
along and the man would give him two
breadcrumbs.
One day the bird felt greedy and he decided to
steal eight breadcrumbs. He put the crumbs in
his nest. The next morning the bird waited until
the man found his last breadcrumb. He slit the
crumb in half and gave the bird one half. When
the bird returned to his nest all of the bread
crumbs had been stolen by a squirrel. Now the
bird only had half a breadcrumb to survive on.

Moral: Don't be greedy.

LAURA REEVES, AGED 9

CHARLEY POWELL, AGED 6

TRAFFIC, TRAFFIC, TRAFFIC

Traffic, Traffic, Traffic,
The air's horrific taste,
The car's all waste.

Traffic, Traffic, Traffic,
One hundred years ago they were under an illusion,
Now the cars have caused pollution.

Traffic, Traffic, Traffic,
As several cars pile up in a prolific heap,
The cars behind inch by inch have to creep.

Traffic, Traffic, Traffic,
Instead of being in an everlasting rat race,
Get some fresh air while walking at a pace.

Traffic, Traffic, Traffic,
A problem of the 20th century,
Can we eradicate this in the 21st century?

NICHOLAS FOSTER, AGED 11

DON'T THROW RUBBISH ON THE FLOOR

Sarah walked past Joe. Sarah dropped some crisp
packets on the floor. She got punished. Her dad
sent her to bed. Now Joe always
puts his rubbish in the bin.

PAUL SMITHERS, AGED 6

I WISH, I WISH

I wish children that have very bad
illnesses could be saved.

CHARLOTTE COPELAND, AGED 11

I wish that people wouldn't live in streets
and they could afford to buy a house.

LUCY SULLEY, AGED 10

THE HORSE AND THE MONKEY

One morning a horse woke up and saw a
monkey. The monkey said, "Watch this, I can
juggle with more bananas than the chimpanzee."
But just then the monkey lost his balance and fell
off the branch. He squashed all of his bananas.
"That's why you shouldn't show off, monkey,"
said the horse.

Moral: Don't show off to others.

JODIE HOWE, AGED 9

THE BIRD IN THE JUNGLE

THERE WAS A BIRD who lived in the jungle with
a lot of other animals and birds. All the other
animals were really brainy and clever. So one day
the bird tried to fly to the top of the tallest tree
in the jungle to show he was clever and he got to
the top. He jumped onto the branch. Because it
was so high he lost his balance and fell off.
The bird died and the other animals laughed.
Moral: Don't pretend to be what you are not.

SARAH RILEY, AGED 8

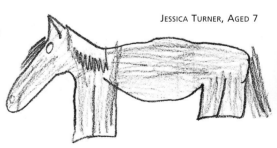

JESSICA TURNER, AGED 7

THE WILD HORSE

The wild horse can run very fast and jump very
high. The horse ran away to avoid man to stay
free and stay alive and to have loads to eat.

Moral: Wild horses should not be caught.

STEFANI TAYLOR, AGED 6

Melanie's Wish
A Fairy Story For The New Millennium

Long ago and far away there lived a young girl called Melanie. She lived on the streets of Scotland. Near where she lived an enormous hill with a grand castle stood. Evella lived there, Melanie's wicked stepmother, the wife of her lovely dad whose life had become a misery.

Melanie's real mum had died about three years ago. She had died of a terrible disease that she caught from dirty animals that roamed around them. Ever since, Melanie had been extremely miserable.

On New Year's Eve 1999, Melanie got taken away by Evella. She accused Melanie of taking some gold from one of her servants. Melanie got locked in a cell. It was horrible, grim and dark. There were creepy crawlies such as spiders, beetles, slugs and snails. There were even some lonely snakes. She was wandering around, thinking extremely hard about how to escape, when she suddenly found a necklace with a diamond on the end of it. It was a lovely green emerald colour and had a gold chain with a clip at the back. In the middle was a picture of the King of Diamonds. She didn't know what to do with it so she just wished a wish and didn't think anything of it until the King of Diamonds spoke back, "Your wish is my command!"

Melanie was astonished. She didn't know what to say. "I would like to make a wish," Melanie blurted out, and then carried on, "My wish is for you to get me out of this place!" "Oh, no. I can't do that, I can't make those kind of wishes come true. Your wish can only be used for the good of all the people in this world for the next Millennium AND it must be wished before midnight!"

"Really?" Melanie was thinking up a cunning plan to get her out of the cell. "What if I give you something?"

"Nope, nothing will do!" The genie wouldn't have it.

"Oh PLEASE!" Melanie shrugged her shoulders.

"Try as hard as you like but I won't grant any wishes that aren't for the good of the world."

"OK. Fine. Be that way," Melanie was quite angry. After a while, she began to realise that it would be quite good to make a wish for the world and she decided to try again with the genie. Just then Evella started coming up the stairs (probably to moan at Melanie again). She

shouted at Melanie for making too much noise (even though she was only trying to get her nightdress on). But then again Evella was always looking for trouble.

Melanie hated being in there. The genie had said that the wish for the future must be used before midnight. There wasn't much time, Melanie thought to herself as she got out of bed. Melanie suggested that the genie called Evella and pretended to be Melanie. He called out, "Evella can you come up here a minute?" They could clearly hear her footsteps coming up. Melanie thought of her as an evil Spice Girl because she always wore big, bulgy black platforms and a short dress, which looked disgusting to her. But when Evella appeared she was not alone. She had two of Melanie's friends with her, Louise and Lucy. They were being put into a cell too. Now it was double trouble!

Melanie had to get herself out, and Louise and Lucy too. There were big heavy metal locks on the doors. She had to work quickly because she had to make her wish in time as well. She started to get to work. First she tried to get open the locks from her cell but time was ticking by. After a while she got it open but realised there were more; one at the top and one at the bottom. But they were quite easy and soon after

she opened the door and she was out! Luckily Evella was asleep. Melanie crept out, first to rescue Lucy. She was there in a matter of minutes and was fighting the locks on Lucy's cell door. But the clock was still ticking! She was soon out, and together they ran at maximum speed to Louise's cell and now they were both at the locks. Soon all three were at the front gates of Evella's castle. Suddenly, the King of Diamond's genie appeared. Lucy and Louise were astonished at the sight they could see but Melanie just said, "How much time left?"

The genie replied, "One minute."

"Hurry up!" shouted Melanie.

"Quickly! Quickly!" added the genie. "5...4...3...2...1!" shouted the genie. And the gates opened. They were free! "And you've got precisely FIVE SECONDS before the wish explodes! So hurry up! Make your wish!" rushed the genie.

Melanie wished "I wish that there were no more people like Evella. I WISH THE WHOLE WORLD WAS GOOD!"

"BANG!" went the wish. And suddenly it was true. The new Millennium had arrived and everything and everyone was good.

Alice Holland, Aged 10

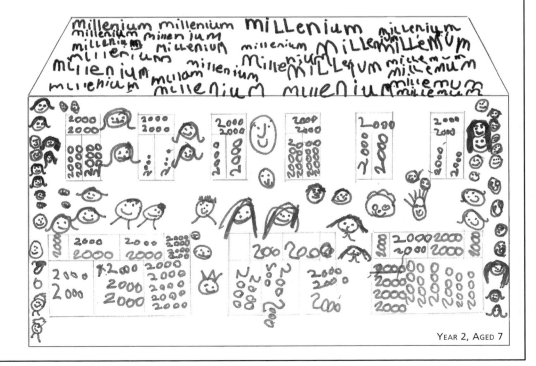

Year 2, Aged 7

PROMISE WISH! SECRETS

My promise is that I would never smoke, even if I got given it, I would not take it. I wouldn't take it if I got given one thousand pounds, I still wouldn't smoke. I think smoking is a waste of money and I don't think it's healthy.

RYAN MCLAUGHLIN, AGED 13

A promise would be if I won money I would give some to charity.

AMY CUMMING, AGED 13

PROMISE (GLOBAL)

I promise to look after the environment by throwing my litter in the bin and not to be lazy by throwing litter on the ground.

PROMISE (PERSONAL)

I promise to do what I can for charity. Whether it be run the London Marathon and be sponsored for it, or if I could get rich I would give some money to charity.

DANIEL SKINNER, AGED 13

My promise is to be good in the year 2000
It's a new start
It's a new leaf
And a new beginning

ROBERT WYNNE, AGED 13

I made a promise to my mum,
That I would always work hard
And stay out of trouble.
At the moment I have done her proud,
Never shouted or been loud,
Tried to keep my excitement in,
And never ever made a sin.

LEE CRASKE, AGED 13

I wish there was no such thing as war and guns and I won the lottery.

CHRIS NEWTON, AGED 12

One day I hope that I will have a good job and good kids, and at my job I get good money so that I can get my kids whatever they want, so they will be happy. That is my wish.

HAYLEY WILLIAMS, AGED 13

My wish is to be a millionaire, have a great job, to be happy and have a nice car.

ROBERT WYNNE, AGED 13

I wish that I had a hundred wishes. With the wishes I would wish that war would never happen and people were always kind to each other. I would wish that I lived in a big house with a swimming pool for the summer. I also wish that people felt safe to leave their doors open when they go out and not be robbed.

SHARRA KENYON, AGED 13

Wishing for a dog
It will be all mine
Still I am waiting
Hearing it barking, it makes me smile

DANIEL LITTELL, AGED 13

I wish in the Millennium that racism will be stopped altogether. I wish that everybody in the world would get along no matter what race or colour they are.

CHRIS MILLS, AGED 13

I have had lots of secrets but I always tell my best friends. One of my secrets is who I fancy. Most of the time I get embarrassed about the whole thing. And most of the time I don't like to tell anybody my secret because it's private and somebody will go back and tell the person and it's not a secret. If somebody goes back and tells, you would not tell them anymore because they will go away and do it again, and if you have a best friend tell them and they would not tell secrets.

NATALIE WEBB, AGED 13

I have had loads of lovely secrets in my life so far. I share them with my little sister and my best friend. My little sister and my best friend tell me their secrets as well. I tell my sister because she never ever tells anybody and my best friend never tells anybody either. I trust my sister and my best friend. My secret is that I never really want to come to school. I would rather go shopping with my family and friends.

TIA STEVENS, AGED 13

Sisters always telling everybody my secrets
Everybody's ears listening about what's being told
Can't they ever stop talking about my secrets
Right I'm fed up I'm telling Mum
Everybody should know some of their secrets
Time for some revenge I say

ROBERT KENT, AGED 13

My secret is my six-month-old brother fell while he was balancing on the floor because I wasn't holding his back properly. He fell down but I was lucky he didn't start crying. If my mum had found out I would have been **DEAD MEAT.**

SAMSON AKANBUKI, AGED 13

KATHERINE REDMOND, AGED 9

SO GLAD THAT I SAID "NO"

"Go on, go on, try a bit,
Go on, you'll be just fine.
These things come quite cheap,
Only ten pounds a time."

I really couldn't believe it.
How could my friends do this?
I didn't want to know drugs,
I wanted to be healthy and fit.

"Oh, come on you wimp,"
They told me,
"It really is so cool,"
And they couldn't even be bothered
To bring themselves to school.

I'm really glad that I said no,
I do feel sorry for my so-called friends,
But I'm <u>not</u> feeling nervous
Or going round the bend.

I'm sitting in the hospital,
Waiting. I'm not ill.
No! I'm waiting for one of my so-called friends.
It was only one little pill.

She's critically ill at the moment,
Lying on a hospital bed.
I wonder if she's going to end up
Being dead.

Moral: Don't be forced to do things against your will.

CLARE HERBERT, AGED 11

THE RABBIT, THE BADGER AND THE PEACOCK

Once upon a time there lived a beautiful peacock. She had a very beautiful tail. There also lived a rabbit and a badger. One day, they both went for a walk. They both saw the peacock's feathers and each wanted one. They thought and thought until they had an idea – they would take a feather from the peacock's tail.

"But how are we going to do that?" asked badger.

"Oh, er ..., we just go behind her and pinch one out," said rabbit. "OK," said badger, "but suppose she feels us pinch it out? She might scream and chase us."

"Oh, that doesn't matter," said rabbit. They sneaked behind the peacock but the peacock turned round and said, "What are you doing behind me?"

Badger said, "We wanted a feather."

"Well why didn't you ask?" said the peacock.

"We were afraid you would say no," said the badger.

The peacock pinched two feathers from her tail. "Here you are," said the peacock.

"Thank you, madam," said rabbit and badger together.

Moral: Sometimes you only have to ask for what you want, so don't steal.

CHARLOTTE JENNINGS, AGED 8

**Save the planet, be aware,
Learn to care and share.**

A MILLENNIUM MESSAGE FROM
THE CHILDREN OF RAGLAN SCHOOL

EDDY'S AMAZING TALENT

One day there was an elephant called Eddy and he lived on an island by himself so he was sad and bored. He lay on his back and pointed his feet up to the sky. He didn't know what to do. He waved his trunk in the air and suddenly it touched some leaves.

"I didn't know I could do that," he said. Eddy thought to himself, "I'd better get off this island and show my friends." So he jumped down into the water. He heard some animals coming towards him and quickly ran to the animals.

They saw Eddie. "Thank goodness, Eddie's coming, hip hip hooray," they shouted. Eddie wanted to show the animals that he had learnt that his big trunk could reach the leaves. Splish, splash, he bumped along the water. And the animals were still coming towards him as he bumped along the water.

They were so happy to see him that they jumped on his back and they cheered three times and once for luck.

"What are you going to show us?" they cried.

"I am going to show you that I have learned that my trunk can reach the highest leaves," said Eddy. "That is amazing!" they all whispered.

"I know," said Eddy, "I only learnt it on that island," he said. "I am so happy that I can do it," he said to himself. "I'm so glad I am me!"

Moral: Be happy with yourself.

BERT TRUBY, AGED 7

Pinocchio

Geppetto made a puppet called Pinocchio when Pinocchio lied his nose grew

Moral: We should not tell lies.

FREDDY KENNY, AGED 5

POEM IN THE STYLE OF JAPANESE KABUKI THEATRE

Murder, killing.
People dying on the streets.
As the war begins.
Your turn.

Murder, death.
So many people are dead.
They are being shot one by one.
Your turn.

We are winning, they are losing.
The nation falls.
The bombers fly past.
Your turn.

We are winning, they are losing.
Now the war has finished.
Now we make up.
Your turn.

Everyone's all right.
Now we shake hands.
Then we give up.
Your turn.

Murder.
                    Death.
Winning.
                    Losing.
Everyone.

End.

TIM MARTIN AND CHRISTOPHER TIDMARSH, AGED 13

MESSAGE SCRATCHED ON A WALL

I hope life has worked out for you. When I was alive I always feared that my memory and my name would fade away, as if I'd never lived. I can tell you now that it doesn't matter if people are going to think of you in the future. If it matters to you, enjoy life while you can. It only comes once. But just so somebody knows my name in five hundred years' time, it's **Thomas Sammarco, aged 16.** I lived, and now so will my memory. Thanks for reading it.

POEM FOR FUTURE GENERATIONS

I'm lying here with you.
I feel relaxed, hot,
nervous and cold.
The world's spinning off its axis.
Who are you? Where are you?

The sky is blue. The sea is calm.
The sun is bright. I wish?
Lucky I am here with you.
Who are you? Where are you?

The sky is black.
The sea's waves are raging
like a ball of fire.
The sun has just gone in.
The night's creatures
are soon to arrive.
Who are you? Where are you?

Don't disappear, I need you.
You give me life and
a reason to live.
You are my dream come true.

I must leave you now.

DOMINIC WHYTE AND
ROBERT WRENCH, AGED 13

HOW TO FEEL HISTORY

Do you want to feel history
From when I was around?
Well, start by picking something
Up off the ground.

A little stone, a simple rock,
Then admire the thing you hold.
Remember every particle
Is a million years old.

As far back as you remember,
And even further on.
It's forgotten up to now
Through all the days gone.

It will be around forever
Through all states of destiny.
It's right there with you in
*   your hand*
But was also around with me.

LUKE CRANENBURGH, AGED 15

IMAGINING YOU

Relaxing so peaceful,
Brilliant the sun beating down,
Seagulls flying round.

Kids screaming, playing,
Beach covered in
beautiful golden sand,
Sunbathing all day.

Swimming in the sea,
Seaweed brushing against my feet,
Paddling through the waves.

Fish sawing repeatedly,
Wonderful, amazing, tickling,
Relaxing in evening sun.

Sun setting slowly,
Down, down,
sun reflecting off water.
Beautiful, joyful.

JAMES BUTT, AGED 13

THE PATH CRUMBLES

THEY LOOK DOWN THE VALLEY below. The ashes are still warm. As they remember the village they used to live in, Larry turned to his sister as she wiped the tears from her eyes. He felt the evening sun on the back of his neck. He turned to face the arrival of night and he said, "Oh, what a world!"

As the night set in, the silvery sun set over the golden valley. The birds sang their final song of the century with full heart. This was a night never to be forgotten and what a beautiful night it was too. It was ironic that the beautiful night was spoilt by the smouldering of the valley.

Decay. Loss. Isolation.

As Larry's sister stood up the sadness was clearly evident. She walked towards the burnt ashes of her treasured village; she broke down into a withering heap of pain and despair. Larry comforted her with care and brotherly love. Everything they owned was gone except for their love for each other. They turned away from the past and headed towards the New Millennium.

BYRON BEARD, ADAM COE AND BEN MANNING, AGED 15

RECTORY PADDOCK SCHOOL

THE LOST CHILD AND THE SPARKLING PURPLE PLANET

Once upon a time there was a sad lost child  who had no name.
One day he found a beautiful, sparkling purple planet.
On the planet, 29 shape children lived in 29 shape houses.

There was no crying and no fighting. They all had fun. The children had beautiful names: **Shaka**, Junior, **Charlotte**, Luke, **Julie**, Brian, **James**, Samuel, **Michael**, Sophie, **Ashley**, Emily, **David**, Jack, **Katie**, Jane, **Dot**, Zakee, **Emma**, Alex, **Jonathan**, Joshua, **Nathan**, Matthew, **Zahraa**, Hope, **Viv**, Doreen and **Michelle**.

"Hello!" said the 29 shape children with 29 beautiful smiles. "Be our friend. Come and see our beautiful planet." It was a special day. It was a happy, happy, happy, happy, happy day. It was the birthday of the purple planet. It was a holiday. The shape children shouted

"Four cheers for the purple planet: hip hip hoi, hip hip hoi, hip hip hoi, hip hip hoi!"
They flew to the clouds, they danced to the hills, they ran to the ocean, they skipped to the river. It was party time.

They picked baked beans from the sky, they drank purple-ade from the river, they poured strawberry milk from the ocean. Butterflies gave them iyan. Purple stew ran from the waterfalls.

Rainbows sent water. Sunflowers gave purple squash. The hills were made of chocolate. In the valley there was an enormous cake with purple icing and these words on top:

"Thank you for our purple planet."
Night came. Candles gave light. It was time to dance. They sang:
"In a circle around and around, In a circle around we go. In and out, Up and down, Now a triangle, Now a star, Clap those hands, Stamp those feet, Joy, joy to all we meet.

Altogether now Shout HOI HOI HOI HOI!"
Where was the sad lost child without a name? They called him TONY. He was as happy as the 29 children. Now there were 30 to take care of the beautiful, sparkling, purple planet.

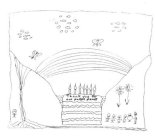

CANARIES CLASS, AGED 5–8

AN ADVENTURE

1
One   day   Emma, Robert, Monim, Charlotte,

Sarah, Gary and Rachael   went   for   a   walk

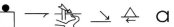
to   the   park.

On   the   way   there   was   a   busy

road   with   lots   of   cars.

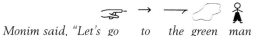
"Stop!" said Rachael. "Cars   can   hurt you."

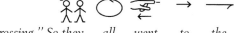
Monim said, "Let's go   to   the   green   man

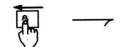
crossing." So they   all   went   to   the

crossing. Emma pressed   the   button.

The   red   man   said   "STOP!"

The   green   man   said   "GO!"

So   they safely crossed   the   road.

SENIOR 1, AGED 11–12

love the earth plant some trees and don't pollute the water. love the animals.. love each other and no fighting. Take care of the world.

MICHAEL SCOTT, AGED 6

RECYCLING

Recycle old papers
Put them in a black box
Watch the men take them away
Into an enormous machine
Swirl and twirl
And squish and squash
Make a gungy soup
Roll it out
Print a paper
SAVE OUR TREES

JACK SHEAD, AGED 7

NICOLA STYLES, AGED 8

TWINKLE, TWINKLE

Twinkle, twinkle, little star,
I do wonder sometimes where you are.
All the smog is killing you,
And all the tall buildings have
    covered you, it's true.

Twinkle, twinkle, little tree,
Where are you for me?
You're going down very fast,
The last tree in the world might be
    a boat's mast.

Twinkle, twinkle, little Earth,
We haven't loved you since your birth.
We're really nasty to this place,
Be nice to it, Human Race.

JESSICA DOLDING-SMITH, AGED 8

CARING

*Caring is important
to everyone. If you
find someone crying
or they have cut their
knee ask them if they
are alright. It will
cheer them up.*

SAM LAWRIE, AGED 7

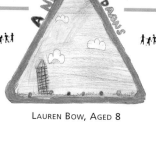

LAUREN BOW, AGED 8

"At Red Hill School we will all endeavour to work together and to be friends"

HELEN EDWARDS, AGED 8

THE GREEDY MONKEY

ONCE A MONKEY was rushing about the trees when he spotted a cup on the ground. He had been fussing about in the trees, so he could not pick it up. He tried but his fingers felt like lead. He called for the snake. "Snake!" he shouted. He only wanted the snake because the cup had some peanuts at the bottom.

The snake came slithering out of the jungle. "You go in that cup and get me those peanuts NOW!" he demanded.

"You can fit your fist in that cup easily," replied the snake.

Wanting to prove the snake wrong, he tried to put his fist into the cup. "It fits!" he shouted in glee. "Now I can eat it all myself."

He tried to pull his hand out. It was stuck! "Oh no!" the monkey cried. "Serves you right for being so greedy" hissed the snake as he slithered off.

KYLIE FENN, AGED 9

Each year of the school has made a contribution to this page.

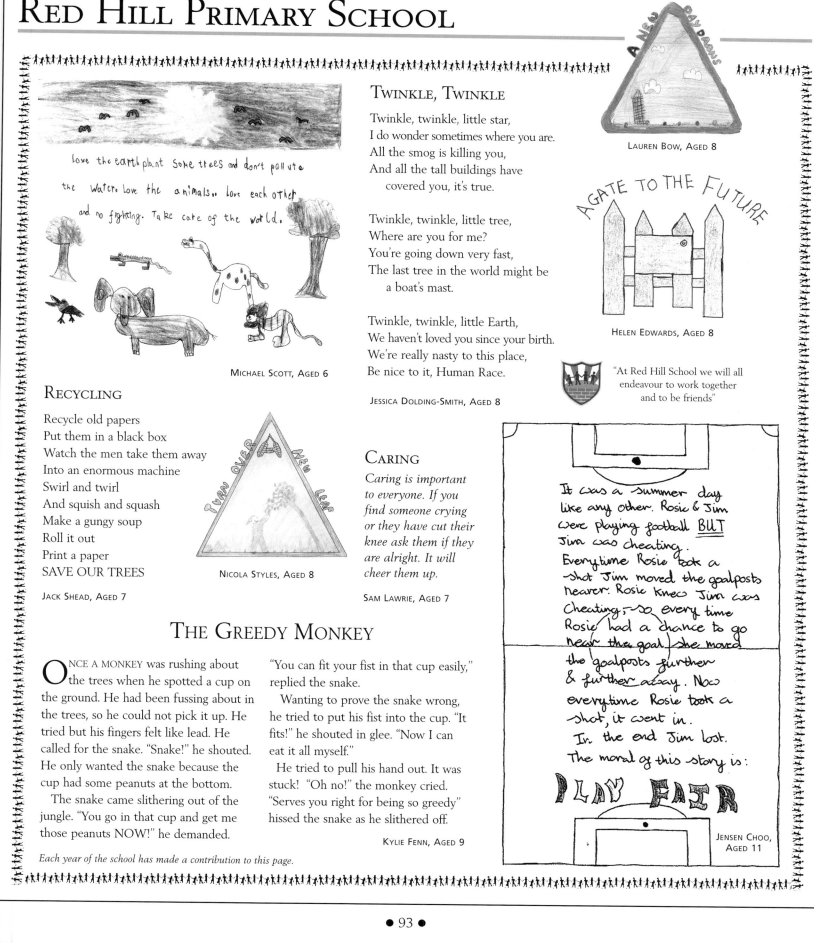

It was a summer day like any other. Rosie & Jim were playing football BUT Jim was cheating. Everytime Rosie took a shot Jim moved the goalposts nearer. Rosie knew Jim was cheating, so every time Rosie had a chance to go near the goal, she moved the goalposts further & further away. Now everytime Rosie took a shot, it went in. In the end Jim lost. The moral of this story is: PLAY FAIR

JENSEN CHOO, AGED 11

Royston Primary School

Ben's Peaceful Place

My fantasy world is where the rabbits hop and the birds sing all day long. There's a golden waterfall and the water is clean, it's the most delicious water anybody could taste. Further through this fantasy world a table stands with a juicy pineapple cut in half, and a cup with fresh orange juice. I walk up to the table…
TEA TIME!

BEN RUSSELL, AGED 8

Will They?

Stripy tiger roars,
Lions explore African plains,
Will they be destroyed?

Wombats are watching,
Koala bears grip the tree trunks,
Will they be destroyed?

Kangaroos follow you,
Monkeys swing on the branches,
Will they be destroyed?

Parrots copy you,
Frogs hop right up to you,
Will they be destroyed?

Bunnies jump up and down,
Moles snuffle around,
Will they be destroyed?

LEANNE SCOLLAN AND MICHELLE ASHTON, AGED 8

The World We Want

We want a sunny, rainy, snowy world,
We want a green world,
With trees, flowers, fishes, and polar bears.
We want jungles,
With frogs, tigers, and green snakes.
We want play houses and toys,
We want people,
Kind, friendly, nice, and polite.

CLASS RJ, AGED 5

The sun is like a big yellow shining balloon.
Bouncing in the sky.

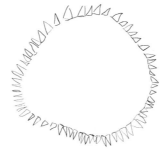

RECEPTION CLASS, AGED 5

LISA BAKER, AGED 10

Earth, sky, sun moon stars
Rainbow over the mountain
Life is beautiful.

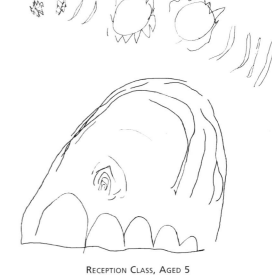

RECEPTION CLASS, AGED 5

Bethan's Peaceful Place

My peaceful place would have trees with blossom, and waterfalls splashing down to the lake. Flowers bloom up out of the ground.

I would be sitting under an oak tree watching the waterfalls and smelling the flowers. In the water fish swim.

Sometimes I would come there with my best friend Megan. We would sit there talking and listening to the birds singing and the squirrels crunching nuts.

No one else knows where this place is.

BETHAN WILKINS, AGED 8

MILLENNIUM

When the Millennium approaches us,
And everybody makes a fuss,
Religion soon is left behind,
But Jesus's heart is good and kind.
It doesn't matter if you're French or Dutch,
Jesus loves you very much,
A Millennium is every thousand years,
So pick up a beer and say,
Cheers!

ANONYMOUS, AGED 11

I wish that in the year 2000 there will be no more nail bombs because lots of people get hurt and die and it's very sad, and before they get to hospital they die too quickly.

ELIZABETH ALLEN, AGED 7

I wish that in the year 2000 there was more equipment for every hospital

EÓIN NESTOR, AGED 7

I wish that there was not any
volcanoes to kill people so they don't die.
Because it will destroy their country
and some policemen will die and
can't save people so they don't die.
Volcanoes are dangerous.

NATHAN ROSWESS, AGED 7

Hello! Our names are Daina, Layla and Amanda. We are in the year 1999. Soon we are going on to the year 2000. When we are in the year 2000 a bug virus will strike some computers. We are remembering the real meaning of the Millennium because 2,000 years ago Jesus was brought into the world. Many cures have been found now, but in the Year 2000 we hope they'll find a cure for the new, rare cancer.

LAYLA MOORE, DAINA TARDIVEL
AND AMANDA PAULEY, AGED 10–11

I wish that in the Year 2000 they stopped cutting
the trees down so if something wrong
happened they could help us live. And if there are
no more trees beavers cannot make their homes
any more. So birds will not be able
to make their nest.

JACK CHANNING, AGED 7

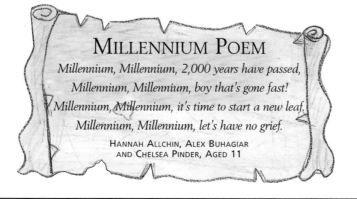

MILLENNIUM POEM
Millennium, Millennium, 2,000 years have passed,
Millennium, Millennium, boy that's gone fast!
Millennium, Millennium, it's time to start a new leaf,
Millennium, Millennium, let's have no grief.
HANNAH ALLCHIN, ALEX BUHAGIAR
AND CHELSEA PINDER, AGED 11

I hope we help the poor people
and make the poor people get rich.

WARREN AUSTEN, AGED 7

I wish in the year 2000 no bombs will be going on because people will die and there will be less people in Brixton. I wish they would stop the bombing in case they bomb our house.

OBINNA MADUAKA, AGED 7

THE YEAR 2000

I wish that in the Year 2000 for the world to have sun and more trees and beautiful flowers and no bad things because the world would be better.

VANESSA PINHAO, AGED 7

I wish that no cats will die because when
you are sad, cats make you happy.

MONIQUE WARD, AGED 7

I Hope

I hope I get a football,
I hope I get a PlayStation,
I hope I get a yo-yo,
I hope I score 100 goals,
I hope I get a teddy,
I hope I …
I hope you think of other people!

O.K.,
I hope for all the refugees,
I hope for people with disease,
I hope these people can find some pleasure,
I hope they can all have fun and leisure,
I hope for peace,
I hope for wars to cease,
I hope, I hope, I hope!

JOHN COLEMAN, AGED 10

A Modern Millennium Miss

The writer of this poem has really ginger hair:
She's cool and she's trendy and really loves to wear
Short tops, pedal pushers, trainers and jeans.
She's really into horses, or so it seems.
She loves playing netball and going to the gym,
And if she's really honest, she thinks she's in.

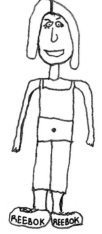

JOANNA HETHERINGTON, AGED 10

HARRIET THOMPSON, AGED 11

Hope

Hope is gold, like the sun.
Hope feels like a refreshing light.
Hope smells sweet, fresh and new.
Hope sounds like happiness
and laughter.
Hope looks like a fresh,
new sunny day.
Hope is new.

JAMES GIN, AGED 10

A Millennium Prayer

Dear Lord,

This Millennium celebrates 2000 years of Christianity. Let us be more grateful for what we have in the years to come and look after your world.

For us, the future looks bright, but for children and adults in some parts of the world it's just the beginning of another era of war and sorrow.

Help us to realise we can make their lives better by supporting charities.

Let the Millennium bring happiness for everyone.

Amen.

ALEXANDRA BAKER, AGED 10

Millennium Bug Causes Devastation

Last night at 12 o'clock, thousands of cheers went up as Big Ben struck 12. Riots broke out, and the police, who were on standby, went into action, closely followed by ambulances and the fire brigade. One officer said: "It was on a far greater scale than we had imagined. People who were drunk started rioting and throwing petrol bombs, and then suddenly all of the electric lights in the city went out."

All The Lights Went Out

A few minutes later, the Y2K, or 'Millennium Bug', kicked into action, stopping the electricity supply and making computers all over the world go haywire. Later on in the night, industrial areas started to suffer explosions, caused by an overload of stress on the machinery, courtesy of Y2K.

RORY ALLFORD, AGED 11

Save Our World's Animals

Over the years many trees and rainforests have been cut down. We must stop this because it is changing our climate and ruining the homes of the animals. Governments should be encouraged to help the environment.

CHRISTOPHER CAMPBELL, AGED 10

MIRIAM KENDRICK, AGED 10

Millennium Messages

I would like the old people to be looked after.

CHLOE WONG, AGED 6

I would like poor people to have food and water.

MILLIE PRICE, AGED 6

I would like everyone to be kind and caring.

ELLIS DAVEY, AGED 7

Look before you leap.

LUCY POWELL, AGED 11

Don't tell lies!
Not even as a joke,
Because they can go horribly wrong!

SARAH FARRELLY, AGED 11

The wolf could not blow the house down.

JESSICA SCOTT, AGED 4

The Crocodile And The Kangaroo

One day a kangaroo said to a crocodile, "I'm faster than you." So the next day they had a Formula One race. In the race the kangaroo went to McDonalds to have a burger. The crocodile went zooming past McDonalds and won.

Moral: Slow and steady wins the race.

JACK SIEBERT, AGED 6

The Boy And The Bear

ONE HOT SUMMER MORNING a boy was walking through the woods when suddenly he spotted a bear. He was mean-looking and he was sitting on a rock eating a poor defenceless rabbit, but as the boy started to run, the bear shouted, "Wait boy, I will not harm you, I am only eating a rabbit because I was so hungry, I didn't have the strength to hunt for fish so I ate a rabbit instead."

When the boy heard these words he started to walk back to the bear and said, "Are you sure you won't eat me?"

"Of course not, all I want is a favour," said the bear.

"What favour do you ask?"

"All I ask is for you to pull out this dreaded tooth, it is killing me. Please pull it out."

"Ok!" said the boy. So he got inside the bear's mouth and tugged on his giant tooth. When the boy pulled it out, before he could climb out the bear slammed his mouth shut and gobbled up the poor little boy.

Moral: Think before you act.

GEORGE VENABLES, AGED 11

Even if something is horrible it is sometimes useful.

JIMMY MAUNSELL, AGED 9

The Lion And The Mouse

One day a mouse was teasing a lion.

"I am going to eat you," said the lion.

But the mouse said, "Please don't eat me. I will help you."

Soon the hunters came and put the lion in a net. Then the mouse came and made a hole, so the lion got out.

Moral: Even if you are small you can still help.

ROBERT BAKER, AGED 6

St James RC Primary School

Snake

The Sun's faint rays strained through
   the curtain of leaves above me,
It was calm and peaceful, like being
   out on a calm sea,
The long grass swayed in the gentle
   breeze like soft rippling waves,
While all around me was a mysterious
   feeling that something amazing was
   about to happen.

Suddenly I heard a rustling from
   behind me, I turned.
A glittering, golden head appeared,
   its gentle beauty,
Broken by two cold black eyes,
Cautiously the snake slithered out of
   the undergrowth,
Quietly flicking its tongue,
Soon its long slender body was shining
   in the Sun's golden rays.

Suddenly the head whipped round,
The snake suddenly became cruel
   and awesome,
It reared up, but suddenly its eyes lost
   their glimpse of courage,
They showed a mix of fear and
   concern,
But the snake soon regained its pride.
An eagle swooped, its talons opened,
   but the snake dodged skilfully.

It tried again, falling quicker and quicker,
I had never felt so powerless,
This time the snake disappeared forever
   into the shadow of the evening,
The mighty eagle had been outdone,
   but still it kept its pride,
So, like the snake, proud and noble,
   it glided away into the evening.

Gemma Slater, Aged 10

The New Baby

My mum brought home a baby today,
I think that it came in the mail,
All I've heard is the sound
   that it makes,
Crash, Bang, Wallop and WAIL!

I don't know where it came from,
Perhaps she got it on sale,
But why can't she take it back now?
Crash, Bang, Wallop and WAIL!

My brother is feeling the strain now,
My mother is looking quite pale,
But because of the noise I can't
   blame them,
Crash, Bang, Wallop and WAIL!

The baby's a little grown up now,
The outlook does not seem so dark,
But my dad brought home
   a puppy today,
CRASH, BANG, WALLOP, BARK!

Gemma Slater, Aged 10

My Holiday In Cornwall

I was on holiday in Cornwall.
We were at the Lizard, walking along
   the grassy cliffs,
Beside the deep blue sea.
It was a hot day so we decided to have a
   drink in a café,
The café was called The Most Southerly Café
   in England.
We sat outside watching the sea lapping,
   gently, against the stony beach.
A notice nearby said,
"Be careful when walking near,
Lots of wildlife lives here,
Adders, rabbits, others too.
If you don't hurt them they won't hurt you."

Not many people were there that day,
As we watched, a silky grey rabbit hopped
   cautiously,
From behind a bush.
It sat listening, then quite suddenly it turned,
It disappeared into the shadows of a tall tree.

"Look quickly over there," Dad whispered,
A magnificent snake slid this way and across
   the grass,
Its scales glinting in the sunlight.
It ignored us although it looked toward us
While heading towards a patch of cool shade.

A passer-by dropped a can into a litter bin,
The snake lifted its head, startled it looked
   around,
Its twinkling eyes darted about the cliff,
In a matter of seconds it had slid away
   out of sight.

Esther Huntington, Aged 10

Rustling Leaves

I'm walking through the forest,
The trees are swaying to and fro from the
   gentle breeze,
An owl hoots but that was all,
Then my heart freezes,
I can hear a slow rustling, weaving through
   the golden
Brown holly leaves on the floor of the forest,
I stand still,
All is quiet,
Then from out of the clearing,
Made by the glistening of the Moon comes
   the snake.
A kind of grey colour, like ash from a spitting fire,
With black, diamond-like shapes black as coal.

It lifts its head and looks in the direction of me,
My nerves are making my heart beat faster
   and faster.

I wish it wasn't there and I was home with my
   hot water bottle in bed,
But seeing it gave me such pleasure,
The beauty of it so spectacular,
And the way it moved.

Just then I moved nearer,
I rustled some leaves with my feet,
The snake looked up suddenly
Slowly, cautiously, curling its body into
   a kind of spiral,
Disappeared into the night air.

Elisa Battista, Aged 10

Marianne's Future

When I think about my life and I look
    into the future,
I see quite a different picture,
From the one I'd like to see.
I would like to see a perfect world,
Like the one that was created.
With food that is good,
And people doing what they should,
And the dodos somehow coming back.
There would be no racism,
No rude words,
And everyone would be treated
    the same.
There would be good education,
And no-one need correction,
This is a good way to live.
Yes if the future was like this,
I surely would give,
My thanks and praises to the one who
    made it this way,
When in the manger Jesus lay,
2000 years to this day.
But like this the future will not be,
So if I keep on being me,
In the future I should cope,
Because I will always have hope.

MARIANNE BUTLER, AGED 10

Christopher's Future

All the cars will be clean
No more parents will be mean
Every child will be glad
And almost never ever sad
No more fatal diseases
No more child's coughs or sneezes
Shopping will be computerized
No more wars between two sides
This is how the future could be
A great place for everyone
Including me
But the choice is up to us
So in ourselves we must trust
Clear up the litter! Clear up the town!
Spread the word up and down
Salvage our food and give what we can
Share everything throughout the land
The future could be a wonderful place
If something is done by the human race!

CHRISTOPHER TWIDLE, AGED 11

The Future

The future decides what happens to me
Huge improvement in this world we will see
Everybody sharing joy or sorrow

Fortune will come to us tomorrow
Upsetting things could happen to us
Take the good and the bad and don't make a fuss
Unforgettable things will always be interesting
Remarkable inventions, bubbling and gurgling
Each one of them will be part of the Millennium

JEFF TONG, AGED 10

Richard's Future

Houses in the sky
Flats up high
Robots doing housework
People being called Perk
Sweets that last forever
People die never
Illnesses treated with care
All animals very rare
That's how it will be!

All toys are electric
So none can take the Mick
Everyone's clothes are designer
People's pocket money go up
    to a niner
People don't go to school
That's the government's rule
Tickets for football matches are free
So that the poor can go to see!
That's how things will be

RICHARD VENABLES, AGED 9

SACHIN ENGINEER, AGED 11

BORDER ILLUSTRATIONS BY SACHIN, MARI, DAN, CHLOE, CHRIS AND PAUL

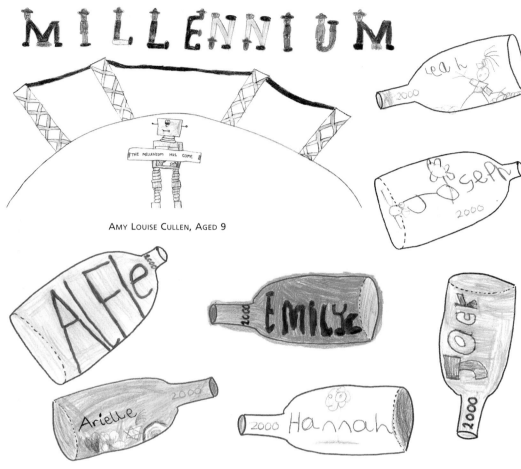

AMY LOUISE CULLEN, AGED 9

ALFIE MAJOR, EMILY CHILDS, ARIELLE FRANCIS, JOSEPH BONNICI, LEAH FIELDING, JACK KNOWD, HANNAH EARDLEY, AGED 4–6

YESTERDAY ... TODAY ... TOMORROW

Yesterday there was no jealousy,
Yesterday there was no hatred,
Yesterday there was no worry,
Yesterday there was no war,
Yesterday there was a future, but now
    that future is gone.

Today we live in jealousy,
Today we live in hatred,
Today we live in worry,
Today some people live in war,
Yesterday there was a future, but now
    that future is gone.

Yesterday the world was full of trust,
Yesterday the world was full of honour,
Yesterday there was no bloodshed,
Yesterday there was a future, but now
    that future is gone.

Today there is no trust,
Today there is no honour,
Today there is bloodshed,
Yesterday there was a future, but now
    that future is gone.

In the future don't let it be the same,
In the future don't let us live in shame,
In the future life shouldn't be a game,
We should try to change our ways, for
    the world is everybody's, not just mine.

TOM HAMILTON, AGED 11

I WONDER IF ...

I wonder if the grass will be green,
I wonder if the world will be clean,
I wonder if aliens will come to Earth,
I wonder if humans will still give birth,
I wonder if we will have a new start,
I wonder if it will be from the heart.

I wonder if the wind will howl,
I wonder how the world will differ
    from now,
I wonder if we'll live on Mars,
I wonder if we will reach the stars,
I wonder if we deserve a new start,
I wonder if it will be from the heart.

SAMANTHA ASHTON, AGED 11

JACK AND JILL

Jack and Jill came down the hill,
    to get a pack of potatoes.
Jack went up the hill,
    to put them in some water.
Jack fell in and hit his head,
    then went to bed.
And Jill ate some Doritos!

ROBERT DONOHUE, AGED 7

In a dark dark place there is a planet, on that planet there is a goblin. in that goblin there is some bones, in the middle of them bones there is a bottle. in that bottle there is a message it says peace

JOSEPH FLANNERY, AGED 7

A Modern Tale Of St George And The Dragon

SME PEOPLE USED only to buy junk food from the supermarket and never ate proper food. Gradually their bodies got weaker. They started developing a new type of cancer. The horrible disease started spreading in the whole town. Like a dragon it was taking one victim every month. One day the most beautiful girl in town also got ill. Her parents were desperate. They announced in the newspapers they would give all their wealth to someone who could save their daughter. Several doctors came and tried to cure her with medicines but the girl was not improving. Then a young doctor named George arrived from America. He fell in love with the girl and decided to do everything to save her life.

Instead of giving her medicines right away like the other doctors, he wanted to find the reason why so many people were getting ill in this town. After some research, Dr George found that everybody who was ill had eaten junk food. He started giving algae and other natural food to the beautiful girl and she got much better. The doctor gave algae to the other people who were ill and they also got better. In this way Dr George managed to beat the horrible disease. Everybody in the town was so grateful and they put a picture of Dr George next to the saints in their church the day when the doctor married the beautiful girl.

IVAN TROEV, AGED 8

The Year 2000

A perfect picture,
Of justice and settlement,
Milleniums gift,
Of whole peace and purity,
Now at truce from war that died.

By
Christopher
Cousins

CHRISTOPHER COUSINS, AGED 11

Thoughts Of The Future

TOBY BARNS WARDA, AGED 7

The New Millennium

ANNIE HORN, AGED 9

Invention For The Future

Wallpaper Painter

ALEXANDRA WATSON, AGED 10

The Millennium Dome

DAISY COSTELLO, AGED 5

Dear God

I wish all the poor people will have some food.
God, I wish all the bad people will be very kind.
I wish all the children and babies were angels.
Thank you for my mother she cares about me.
Thank you for food, for as I know.
Some people don't have any food.
Amen.

NEIL PAVITT, AGED 6

Cleaning And Clearing In The 21st Century

DUST DOME

This is what the "Dust Dome" looks like when not in use !

The "Dust Dome" is programmed by an in-built computer.

The hose is extendable.

This invention is based on the millennium dome

Cordell Coster, Aged 9

Washing Machine
The talking Wash-o-matic machine !

The price is right for you !

Only £500 !

You talk to this machine and it will talk to you !

Latest technology – every housewife will want one of these !

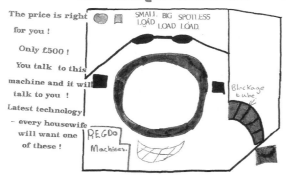

Jake Crawford, Aged 10

Wheelomatic
When The Eye Flashes 1/2 Red & 1/2 Blue, It Means That It Has Broken Down

Oliver Goodall, Aged 9

CHEWY CHARLIE THE WONDER WASHER!!!

PUT THE CLOTHES IN IT'S MOUTH.IT WILL CHEW THE WASHING TO MAKE IT CLEAN.

ALL CIRCLES AND SQUARES ARE BUTTONS FOR:ON, OFF ,FULL AND HALF FULL.

IF DIRT GETS BLOCKED,CHARLIE WILL WASH IT OUT OF A TUBE.

PRICE:£158.99!!!!

WHEN CHARLIE SAYS "DONE" ,THE WASHING COMES OUT OF A DRAW AT THE FRONT.

Lacey Withers, Aged 8

HOUSEHOLD ROBOT
This robot is specially made for all your household needs

Daisy Robson, Aged 10

A FUTURISTIC WASHING MACHINE WITH AUTOMATIC POWER SYSTEM AND AUTOMATIC DRYING

The washing machine will wash your clothes for you. When they are dry, the washing machine will automatically put them on the line. When they are fully dry, the machine will fold the clothes up, then it will drop them into the basket.

THE FUTUREMATIC

Lauren Sherwood, Aged 9

The Dry-o-matic

The "Dry-o-matic" has a special heat beam, that gets your washing dryer than any other machine on the market !

Price £300 Only !

This price is the lowest ever and we will guarantee a quality after sales service!

Sam Wynne, Aged 10

Washing Machine — Wash day in the future

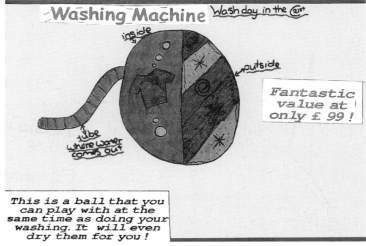

Fantastic value at only £99 !

This is a ball that you can play with at the same time as doing your washing. It will even dry them for you !

Rachel Matthews, Aged 9

ST PAUL'S WOOD

Saw poppies swaying in half-wild fields
Took photographs of ruined rusty cars.

Puddles of paint forming slowly on the ground
And a crane came to take the cars away
Underfoot glass smothered the ground
Litter sprayed all around
Spectacular views surround.

Wildlife can be found
Occasional horses trot into sight
One with a foal
Do look after St Paul's Wood and help to improve it.

LUCY HARRIS, AGED 11

My Lovely Horse.

My lovely horse
I love you very much.
my lovely horse
you are very polite.
my lovely horse.
I like your coat.
My lovely horse
I love your dancing.
my lovely horse
carried me away
To a lovely land.
my lovely horse
I loved that day.

GEMMA DANIELS, AGED 6

What is blue

What is blue?
The sea is blue
with little fish swimming through.

What is white?
A sheep is white
on the hill side at night.

What is red?
A lady bird is red
sitting on a flower bed.

What is yellow?
A sun flower is yellow
growing in the Meadow.

DANIELLE RUDKIN, AGED 7

What IS BLUE?

What is blue?
The waters blue
in the rivers ending.

What is white?
A polar bear's white
In the North Alantic

What is red?
A fires red
IN Central London.

What is gold?
The stars are gold
Twinkling in the
Night time.

What is yellow?
The sun is yellow
Shining in the days
Passing.

STEVEN COPE, AGED 7

DAZED

Sitting under the baking sun,
Chewing a hot-cross bun,
I, for no reason, decide to go for a walk,
Under the baking sun.

Walking under the baking sun,
My walk is almost done,
But then, as I near the peak of a hill,
A burst of colour fills my eyes.

Dazed under the baking sun,
The flash of colour gets clearer in my mind,
Until I realise what I'll have to find,
A field of golden daffodils,
Standing there before me.

The King and Queen,
The tallest of them all,
Are guarded by a hundred knights,
And on the outside, the trumpeters announce
The arrival of the Royals.

Suddenly I wake up
From my daydream,
But still, on the peak of the hill,
Sitting next to the golden beautiful scene.
I go home, no thought entering my head,
Except for the crowd of daffodils,
Although I cannot see them anymore,
The vision will stay with me forever.

EDWARD HICKS, AGED 10

DANIEL DIXON

St Philomena's RC Primary School

My Prayer For The Millennium

Dear God,

Please stop all wars. Why can't they just be friends and stop fighting?

For the year 2000 may people make something else rather than make war. Stop people wasting money on bombs and weapons and give it to the poor.

Help us to do more for others and to love one another as you love us. Please help doctors to find a cure for cancer and also for meningitis.

Amen..

EMILY MYLES, AGED 7

*We wish for lots of things but, most of all,
we wish that everyone in the world had
clean water and somewhere to live.*

CLASS 1, AGED 4–5

Love Or Money

My Mum once sung me a song when I was feeling sad. It went "Love can build a bridge," and I have always remembered it even though it was a few years ago. Even when I can't afford some things but others can, I don't strop. I just sing that song to myself. You may not always have money, but you will always have love.

MATTHEW CONLAY, AGED 11

PETER LEE

EMILY FOORD

*I wish every country had food,
Then everybody will be well,
And everybody won't be dead.
God will look after them.*

DANNY BOTTING, AGED 5

Life In The Year 2999

Bow**L**ing balls floating
M**E**teorite strike
Tenn**I**s on the moon
Shooting at the Sun
Universal football league
Sco**R**ing amongst the stars
Ali**E**ns eat the ball
(Oops, they won the cup!)

Hover home
Fl**O**ating
To the **M**oon
Upsid**E** down
Stars at breakfast

Vast time-**T**ravel with
Nifty **R**ocket cars
Smooth **A**eroplanes
Chasing **V**irtual quads
As el**E**ctronic pods
Move in **L**iquid tunnels

Funky feather dresses
Chocol**A**te hats
Sun**S**afe swimming costumes
Fas**H**ion shows on Mars
F**I**reproof pants
Rocket-p**O**wered trainers
Air-co**N**ditioned socks
(no more smelly feet!)

YEAR 4, AGED 8–9

The Time Capsule

GREETINGS to whoever finds this chest. We have made it into a time capsule and have included some of the things that we have in our world at the start of the New Millennium.

Many animals are in danger of extinction, such as pandas, tigers and elephants. We hope that they are still alive when you read this letter but, in case they are not, we enclose some pictures of them.

Many rivers have been polluted. We hope that a way has been found to stop this happening.

We have put in some of the money we use today. There is talk of everyone using the Euro as currency in the New Millennium, so perhaps you have not seen this money before.

Our country is ruled by a government and we have a Royal Family. The Queen is Queen Elizabeth II. You can see her on some of the coins we have put in the chest. Is Prince William King of England now?

Some of our favourite hobbies are reading books, football, hockey, horse riding and swimming.

We also like to listen to cassettes and CDs. We have put a Discman and some CDs in. The most popular singers at this time are Britney Spears, Bewitched, Cartoons, Boyzone, Westlife, Cher and Steps.

Our wish for the future is that the world is a happy, peaceful place with no illness or poor people.

YEAR 3, AGED 7–8

MAIRTIN DWYER

STEPHANIE CATER

SAM WARNER

A Donkey In Borrowed Fur

THERE WAS ONCE A DONKEY whose name was Ienaphets. He lived in a hut in a deserted corner of the forest of Retac. The forest of Retac was in the land of Harobed, which was ruled by a lion and a council of owls.

Now, the reason he lived in an almost deserted area of Retac was because he was very shy and very timid. He had nothing to help him get braver as he was too shy to make friends.

After several years of isolation, Ienaphets decided that he was brave enough to go for a walk. On this walk Ienaphets found a lion skin. He took it home and draped it over his shoulders. It was a perfect fit. He looked just like a King himself.

When he went on further walks, he went about making everyone believe that he was a King. (The real King had gone on a year's holiday in Barbados, which none of the animals, except Ienaphets knew about so none of the animals knew any better.)

This went on for several months and the animals began to get suspicious because Crow thought that he saw the skin slip.

One day, Crow went to see Ienaphets and found him asleep. Crow looked around and saw the skin on the floor beside Ienaphets' bed of hay. Crow noted this and went to report to the other animals.

The animals decided to put the 'King' to the test. They decided to ask the 'King' to hunt and kill another animal for they knew that would solve the mystery. They put Ienaphets to the test and, surprise, surprise, he failed.

The next morning, Ienaphets, dressed as the lion, went outside to find that he was surrounded by other animals.

They said, "Give up Ienaphets! We know that you are playing a game. We have contacted the real King and he said that you are banished from Harobed. So pack your bags and go! You are no longer wanted here."

Moral: Never try to be someone you're not because you'll always get caught out.

STEPHANIE CATER, AGED 10

Millennium Thoughts

The children are outside
watching their bonfire
sizzling, snapling, crackling.

The massive crowd gathered
around the Dome,
Celebrating, dancing, singing
and feasting as they roam.
Counting down to the midnight
hour, the clocks tick tock.
Big Ben's bells ringing loudly,
Crowd and children cheering
gladly,
Fireworks in the night sky
exploding brightly.
With celebrating, the
century begins.

But back then, at the stable
behind the Inn,
Sleeping peacefully baby Jesus
just born in Bethlehem.
Let's remember him
this Millennium.

STEPHEN REILLY, AGED 9

Millennium Prayer

Thank you for the time,
When I saw my cousin,
For the first time.

TANYA PATEL, AGED 6

You never know when the clock might stop. The clock of life is wound but once. Every minute you're ageing, you never stop. Every day your death might come for the clock of life is wound but once.

Thank you God for the
times I was happy,
Thank you Jesus for
the times I was sad,
Thank you God
for sending your son,
And thank you for the
Millennium.

KATIE NICOLSON, AGED 7

GERARD KELLY, AGED 10

Thank You

Thank you Father for
the gift of time.
Time is very valuable.
God does not want you
to waste it.
Thank you for the gift of
January 1999.
January is the month when
Mrs Wright became our
new head teacher.

Thank you Father for the gift
of September 1999.
Autumn starts in September.
The leaves fall in different
colours.

EXTRACT FROM A POEM BY
CLAIRE SHEEHY, AGED 8

Dear God

Please help all the people who are sick.
When I grow up I want to be a nurse.
Please let me look after the people in hospital.
I will look after animals as well.
Amen.

ROSIE HENNESSY, AGED 5

HOLLIE HENNESSY, AGED 5

Everyone Is Good At Something

HAZELNUT GREEDILY MUNCHED his lettuce, looking around for some more of the crunchy, green leaves. His nose twitched every so often. He was really rather a common looking young rabbit with matted, brown ochre coloured fur. One of his ears stuck up and the other flopped down awkwardly. Around him, twenty tired rabbits were eating radishes and munching lettuce too. A few yards away, a small rabbit peeked out from the warren hole below the old oak tree and cautiously, paw by paw, climbed out and hastily nibbled a morsel of rosy red radish from the grassy ground in front of him. The rabbit's name was Blackberry. He was a timid little rabbit and scampered off when anything approached him. His fur was very silky and white with large, ebony black markings that looked like big, juicy blackberries ready to eat! He had a white powder puff tail and his huge, floppy ears dangled over his shiny, blue eyes and almost covered them completely! He was really rather handsome and very appealing.

Hazelnut was very envious of Blackberry's fine looks. Not only that, Blackberry was the most intelligent young rabbit in the whole of the Radish Burrow (the school for young rabbits). This made Hazelnut even more jealous. He always scored the lowest mark in the class tests. He could be a right old bully and particularly enjoyed picking on Blackberry even more than the other rabbits whom he would often tease by hitting and biting for his own amusement.

It was a bright, sunny day in the summer term when the rabbit pupils were sitting their last Animal Test. Blackberry was happily scribbling down the answer to the last question, when Hazelnut came over. A naughty smirk lurked on his face and there was a glint of spitefulness in his eye. "Look who it is! It's that old smarty pants, Blackberry – or should I say Smarty-berry!" teased Hazelnut doubling up with laughter and rolling around so much that his fur got covered in dust! He grabbed Blackberry's test book and ripped it to shreds. He kicked the tiny ripped pieces of paper out into a muddy dark tunnel and left them there, bounding off quickly with his friends. Blackberry's teacher was furious! He blamed Blackberry who was too upset to do the test all over again.

Afterwards, Blackberry burst into bitter tears. He couldn't take any more of this teasing! What was he to do?

The answer came in an unexpected way at the Rabbit Races Sports Day the following week. Although rather common looking and not very good in class, Hazelnut was a brilliant athlete. He could run so fast you would have thought he was a rocket! He disappeared in the blink of an eyelid! He could jump so high, you would have thought he had springs in his legs!

Hazelnut ran his first race eagerly. His large paws padded along the field at supersonic speed! It was not surprising that he won all the races easily. "Hooray for Hazelnut! The Champion!" cheered the rabbit spectators. Hazelnut was so proud of himself. Walking up to the podium, he beamed as he was awarded his gold medal. He really was rather proud and conceited, sticking his nose in the air, silently boasting.

Meanwhile, having lost all his races, Blackberry had just slunk away into his classroom in the third burrow. His teacher, who was already there, informed him that he had scored full marks in his last Animal Test. But poor Blackberry felt so depressed, he didn't listen.

At that moment, Hazelnut burst into the classroom, still feeling full of himself. He caught sight of Blackberry's long, glum face. It was then that he realized how awful he'd been to Blackberry. Hazelnut's friend had been so happy and proud of him at the races, but when Blackberry had done really well in class, all he, Hazelnut, had done was to scoff and spoil it for him.

Hazelnut pondered for a moment. He now understood that there was no need to be jealous of Blackberry. He should be proud of what Blackberry could do, just like his friends had been proud of him for what he could do. After all – everyone is good at something, so we should be proud of each other, and not jealous!

SUSANNAH TURNER, AGED 10

The Bad-tempered Crocodile

There was once a very bad-tempered crocodile who always splashed the other animals that drank at the pool where he lived. He used his big strong tail to splash them.
The zebra, lion, elephant, and snake were fed up with the crocodile and decided to teach him a lesson, so snake made herself look like a crocodile by sticking lots of leaves from the jungle onto her long body. Snake slid into the pool and began splashing the bad tempered crocodile.
"Stop, stop!" said the crocodile.
Snake said that she would stop only if crocodile promised not to splash anyone else who came to the pool. Crocodile agreed because he had learnt that if you are unkind and bad tempered towards someone else and they do it back to you, it isn't very nice.

RECEPTION CLASS, AGED 4–5

SOUTHBOROUGH PRIMARY SCHOOL

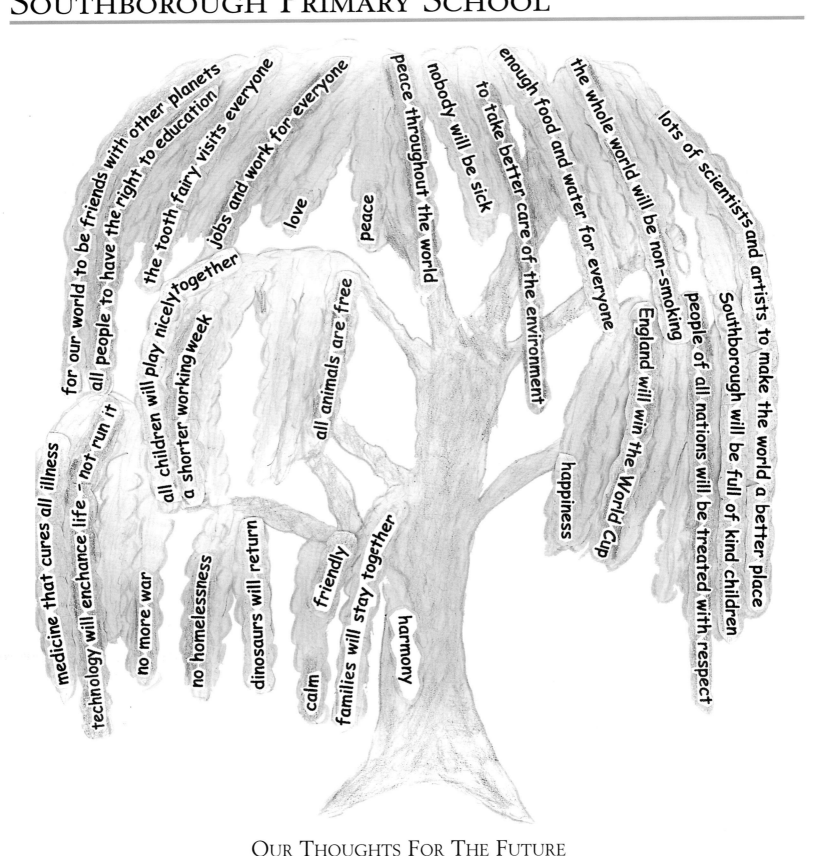

for our world to be friends with other planets

all people to have the right to education

the tooth fairy visits everyone

jobs and work for everyone

love

peace

peace throughout the world

nobody will be sick

to take better care of the environment

enough food and water for everyone

the whole world will be non-smoking

lots of scientists and artists to make the world a better place

all children will play nicely together

a shorter working week

all animals are free

people of all nations will be treated with respect

Southborough will be full of kind children

England will win the World Cup

happiness

medicine that cures all illness

technology will enchance life – not run it

no more war

no homelessness

dinosaurs will return

calm

friendly

families will stay together

harmony

OUR THOUGHTS FOR THE FUTURE

THE CHILDREN OF SOUTHBOROUGH PRIMARY SCHOOL, AGED 5–11

Tubbenden Infant School

Millennium Thoughts

In the Millennium I think that computers will be much more sophisticated. Children will use modems day and night.
GAVIN TAYLOR, AGED 7

In the Millennium we will wear pretty green make-up that tastes of cucumber.
SAMANTHA REID, AGED 7

I hope that people's lives will be better and that my town will smell like strawberries.
BETH ROGERS, AGED 7

Cars will fly with special engines! There won't be planes, there'll be spaceships. Instead of Biggin Hill airport there'll be Biggin Hill spaceport.
ANDREW DUFFIELD, AGED 7

I wish my fork could feed me,
I wish I could dye my hair green,
I wish a prince would rescue me.
DEMI ROSE, AGED 7

I think that in the Millennium space will be different because there will be new ways of getting about. There could be new spaceships that could go out of this galaxy! There might even be cities on the Moon. We could bring up bricks and cement from Earth so we could build a space town! When we wanted to go on holidays we could go to Mars or Pluto. That would be fun because we would see if aliens were real!

KATIE HASLINGDEN, AGED 7

To dear Salonee, my baby sister,

I am writing to you to tell you what it will be like in the Millennium. There will be computer-driven cars so you will not have to look where you are going! But, Salonee, that's not all. In the year 2000 you won't have to go to school because Mum or Dad will teach you at home with SATs Discs and English Discs on the computer.
Love, Prianka.

PRIANKA JAMNADAS, AGED 7

In The Year 2000

In the next year
Maybe something queer
Will take place
In the Human Race
Such as
Fishes that grant wishes!
I don't know
I'm only guessing
Maybe it's true

ROSIE OWEN, AGED 7

In the Millennium,
Every single thing will be
UPSIDE DOWN.
Schools will be under water,
People will live underground,
Trains will fly through the air,
In the Millennium.

JAMES THOMAS, AGED 7

TAK KATO, AGED 7

Me And The Millennium

In the future it will all change. Trains will fly like birds. Schools will be palaces and we will always be Princes and Princesses. I wish, I wish, I could always be a baby.

ABIGAIL BOTT, AGED 7

Millennium Promises

When my baby sister grows up in the 21st century, I promise not to boss her about.
BRITTANY PUMMELL, AGED 7

I promise to try to stop men from killing the biggest tigers because they are my favourite animals.
REBECCA ARNAUD, AGED 5

I promise that in the Millennium I will help stop starvation in Africa.
JOSEPH GALVIN, AGED 7

I promise to go to bed and put my pyjamas on without being told.
EMILY HUDSON, AGED 5

I promise to exercise hard.
ROSS MARSHALL, AGED 5

I promise to wash the car, Dad.
SHEVANNAH MULCAHY, AGED 5

I promise to look after my friends when they have got no one to play with.
ZOE JACKSON, AGED 5

I promise I will help Mummy to do the washing up.
LUCY DESBOROUGH, AGED 5

I promise to care for all animals.
BETHANEY GIBBS, AGED 5

I promise to eat less sweets.
DANIEL CROCKETT, AGED 5

I promise to be kind to all my friends.
THOMAS PARRY, AGED 5

I promise to work hard at football and play for ENGLAND.
MICHAEL LAMB, AGED 5

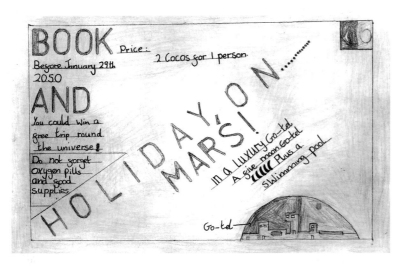

BOOK
Price: 2 cocos for 1 person.
Before January 29th 2050
AND
You could win a free trip round the universe!
Do not forget Oxygen pills and food supplies

HOLIDAY ON MARS!
In a luxury Go-tel
A five moon Go-tel
Plus a swimming pool

Go-tel

WILLIAM BISHOP, AGED 9

SOME OF MY WISHES

I hope that in the next Millennium some extraterrestrial life of some sort will be found, even if it's only bacteria. I also hope there will be a manned expedition to Mars. I hope there will be less pollution and more people will walk to work. All the pollution that was made will be disposed of into something like what astronomers call a black hole. These are some of my wishes for the next Millennium.

MARK DARLING, AGED 8

MY DIARY, 7TH MAY, 3064

Today is Thursday and we had our Martian Maths test. I was terrified but then afterwards we had a great time in our terrifying tests for Holographic Teachers class, which is where our teachers who are holograms have tests and it's funny because they get muddled up. I hate Martian Maths tests though, because it's a test in the Martian form of language. Blasting Biology was next. It was excellent. It's biology basically, but most times something goes wrong and it goes BANGOREG! So we call it Blasting Biology. We did Enchanting English, which is where all the stories come true. Then we did Raging Reading, which is where words fly around the room and we have to read them. The only thing is it makes you go like Dizzy Lizzy because they go so fast.

CLAIRE SMITH, AGED 9

THE TELEPORTER

The Teleporter is a machine that can change your life by getting you from one place to another, like from your home to Japan, all you would have to do is use the Teleporter. This gadget can save you a long journey to wherever you want to go. The electricity in this machine will last up to 40–45 years. If you want to get somewhere quickly, it will get you there in 2.5 seconds.

MATTHEW ADAMS, AGED 11

MY TIME CAPSULE FOR THE NEW MILLENNIUM

My computer and some CDs would go in because they might want to know what we used, each type of coin and note in case money is different in a thousand years, my recorder so they know what sort of instruments we play today, books, true stories and fantasy stories, to show our language, videos to see what entertainment we have, a picture of my house so that they know what kind of places we live in.

JENNIFER SPENCER, AGED 9

Teddy bear
'Girl Talk' magazine
Computer game
Sewing and weaving
A poem
Crystals
Playstation
China doll
Beanie baby
My diary
Money

HANNAH RAY, AGED 9

I HAVE A DREAM

I have a dream that in the next Millennium poverty will end and the needy will be provided for. The homeless will have homes, the hungry will have food, the thirsty will have water. Let the wealthy be generous, let the poor be respected.

I have a dream that wars will end and peace will reign. Munitions will cease to exist and the only conflicts between humans will be those by word of mouth.

I have a dream that the next Millennium will bring an end to racism. No-one will be judged by their looks but by their personality and character. Please God, let humans live with equal rights and in harmony.

ALICIA TEW, AGED 11

VALLEY PRIMARY SCHOOL

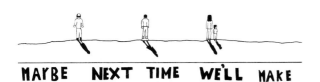

MARK BRAZIER, AGED 10

HOW WE CAN HELP

I can help dry the dishes.
I can help my friends.
I can help my younger brother.

RECEPTION CLASS, AGED 4–5

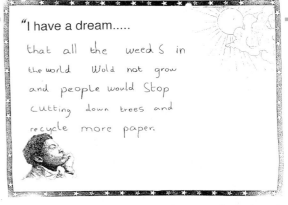

ALEXANDER CLARK, AGED 6

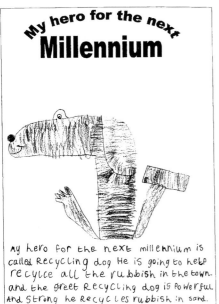

My hero for the next millennium is called Recycling dog He is going to help recycle all the rubbish in the town. and the great Recycling dog is Powerful And strong he recycles rubbish in sand. He like to save Rubbish.

SAM RETTER, AGED 7

AN ENDING FOR THE PRINCESS AND A FROG

ONE DAY the Princess broke her promise with a frog. She ran off to the Palace. When she got there she heard a knock on the door. "Who can that be?" she said. It was a frog. "Who are you?" said the Princess. "I'm a frog." "Go away," she said. When they were all asleep the frog came. The Princess woke up. The frog said, "Can I get into your bed?" "Yes," she replied. When the frog got into bed, he turned into a Prince. And then the witch came and turned everyone into a frog and they never lived happily.

FRED ALLEN, AGED 5

ANNIE KATCHINSKA, AGED 8

THE LUCKY FOXES

Friday 22nd January, 1999

LONG AGO FOXES WERE CHASED for their skins. Then one day two foxes were being chased by the people who sold animal skins when suddenly one of the men jumped out in front and almost got them, but they quickly managed to escape through the man's legs. They ran and ran as fast as they could, then they quickly jumped into a bush at the side. There they saw two lost children. The children saw the two foxes and said, "Hello." The foxes said "Hello" back to the children. They asked the foxes what was wrong. The foxes explained everything and so did the children. The foxes told the children that their names were Foxy and Loxy. The children told the foxes that their names were Simon and Charlotte and that their parents were King and Queen.

Then the children told the foxes that they were lost. Then Foxy and Loxy said, "We'll try and get you home." "Thank you very much," said the children. So they started on their way. They were walking along talking about where they lived. They went round corners and bends making their way up as they went. They came to a river that had crocodiles in it, but there were stepping stones as well. Luckily the crocodiles were asleep. So they crept over, but the crocodiles started snapping so they quickly ran across. They survived. They were out of breath when they got across but they carried on walking close together. Simon and Charlotte got very scared. Then suddenly a big "roaaaaar!" came out of the bushes, Oh no! It was a lion. "Quick, run!" said Foxy. They were running as fast as they could, the lion was right on their tail. They came to a dead end. Charlotte said, "Oh no!" Now what should they do? The lion was getting closer. There was a tree right behind them so they quickly climbed up it, the lion jumped and only just missed them. They stayed up the tree until the lion had gone. Five minutes later ... finally, the lion had gone. So they came down. As they walked on it became foggier and foggier, they took one more step, yuck! They had

stepped into a swamp with even more crocodiles. They quietly crept across, luckily they were all right, so they went on. The people who were always chasing them, found them and started chasing them. They ran and ran as fast as they could. Simon and Charlotte started to recognise some of the way home because their mother took them for a walk every day. They had an idea, they ran into the Royal Garden. The bad people stopped and tried to run away but the guard closed the gates. The children were so pleased to be back and the King and Queen were so pleased to have them back. The children told their parents about how the foxes had helped them and been so brave and what had happened. So the King said the foxes are no longer to be chased and they can live free and wild. As for the animal skin people, they were put in prison. That's why foxes are wild today.

Moral: Do a good deed and you will receive one back.

SADIE EXFORD, AGED 10

THE SOLUTION THAT SAVED THE ELEPHANTS

THE EARTH TREMBLED as another elephant fell to the ground: Dead. The hunters slowly surged towards the elephant, shrieking with laughter. While, far away, safe under the trees, the herd to which the elephant once belonged, watched its painful death.

Quietly the elephants crept to the lake. Tarquin was fed up. He was the leader, so he called for a meeting, as they needed to get to the top of the volcano Salamandastron where they could summon up their god, Saxtus, who they hoped would stop this killing. It was decided that Tarquin would go to the top of Salamandastron where he could summon Saxtus.

By noon he was at the tip of the woods, but any further and he would be seen by the hunters and shot. He decided that he would rest there until midnight, when he would sneak across the clearing to the woods which surrounded Salamandastron.

At midnight he did what he had planned until he fell into a trap and his leg was caught in some rope. The elephant went berserk!

His mind was filled with rage. He swung his trunk around and sliced the rope in two. He rested until daybreak to recover, then the herd leader slowly stumbled up the volcano. Sometimes he rested in caverns in the rocks. Suddenly a storm came upon him, and as he still walked the winds pulled him back and the water tried to sweep him off his feet, but he carried on.

There was a roar, the volcano erupted and lava oozed down the mountain. Tarquin carried on. Then chunks of rock hit him and blocked his path but whilst his skin burnt, his feet still stinging, he raised his mighty trunk and pushed the rocks out of the way. Tarquin carried on.

Finally he reached the top. With all the power left in him he cried, "Lord Saxtus, help me and my herd. Hunters are killing us one by one." Tarquin fell to the ground, exhausted, dead.

Saxtus heard his cry and where the hunters were camping the earth opened and they fell, till the ground closed around them and crushed them.

Where Tarquin lay, the ground eventually covered him up and beautiful flowers grew there and it became a place where elephants would always be protected. All around the world today Tarquin helps elephants who are being hunted down like his herd had been. His name will never be forgotten.

DAVID WALSH, AGED 10

MY GIFT TO THE MILLENNIUM

I will put in my gift
A feather from a garden gnome,
Some magic words of a genie from a lamp,
A golden blade of grass.

I will put in my gift
A slippery surface of silver sap,
A lake of lilies on little lily pads,
Some golden dawn of the morning.

I will throw away
The evilness and greediness,
And selfishness to animals.
I will throw it in a deep, dark cave.

I will wrap my gift up
in glittering stars,
And kindness from the Moon.
I will tie it up in a ribbon,
Made from the clear, deep ocean waves.

I shall fly on silver wings
To Heaven and give my gift to God,
Who will sprinkle it over the world
To share kindness, a good thought
Between me and you.

JENNIFER NICHOLLS, AGED 8

FOR THE MILLENNIUM

I promise to be friends with everyone.

LAURA NICHOLLS, AGED 5

DEAR LORD

Please let all families have shelter and food and water so people won't be hungry or thirsty. Can you try to make people understand not to fight? Give money to poor people so they can buy seeds to grow, spades and shovels, and plant pots. Please let the poor people go to school.
Amen.

CHRISTOPHER DOBSON, AGED 6

I wish people would be kind to animals.

ALICE BLACKSHAW, AGED 5

THINK OF THE WORLD

Think of the world long ago,
When pollution wasn't there.
What happened to
the world of ours?
When we weren't always there.

Think of all the animals,
Even the ones in the sea.
When the oil is spilling,
Where should we be?

Think of the flowers and trees,
That are in our parks.
Where shall we always be?

Saving our world!
Come save with us.

EMILIE HARRIS AND
SARAH IVINGS, AGED 9

I wish I could fly like Peter Pan.
I wish there was clean water for everyone.

JACK REGAN, AGED 6

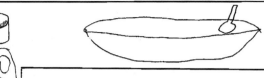

MILLENNIUM MIX
A recipe for the future
Ingredients:
20 litres of kindness
50 litres of information
200 tablespoons of help
700 kilograms of care
7 tablespoons of love
90 kilograms of clear air
10 tablespoons of tolerance
60 litres of generosity

Method:
Put help and tolerance into a very
large bowl and mix well. Pour kindness
and generosity and information in the large
bowl as well and stir with the help of tolerance.
Put clear air and love and care in the large bowl
as well and mix it all together for 2 months.
Cook in a cool oven for a week. Then ice
it with care and sprinkle it with love.
Then share it with the rest of the world.

FRANCESCA NORMAN, AGED 7

I wish we had food and
water for everyone.

POLLY KISSOCK, AGED 5

POLLUTION

We wreck the land around us,
killing creatures in our path,
machines come and dump
sour smelling rubbish in holes.

We throw our litter
wherever we please,
we don't care at all,
things are dying everywhere,
it's all our fault.

We drive our cars round every day,
giving off fumes,
factories working,
people smoking,
skies turning black.

Mankind will never learn,
polluting is no fun,
the air is getting hard to breathe,
what have we done?

JAMES CAMPBELL MACDONALD, AGED 9

I would like people to stop cutting trees down

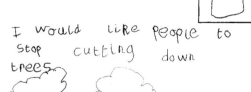

JAKE GARLICK, AGED 5

When I grow up
I want to be kind.
I wish the world
wasn't smelly.

CHARLIE AUSTIN, AGED 6

I would like the wars to stop

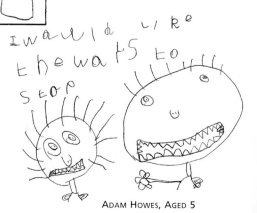

ADAM HOWES, AGED 5

A Promise For the Future

I was a little boy and I'm 7 years old. I have a promise about there is going to be nice clean rivers and sea and water that is clean to drink and bath with

By Stephen Fisher 7 years old

My **wish** **for** **the** **Year**

My Wish fon the yean

2000.

2000

I **wish** I could go to the

Gneek islands fon all

my holidays.

JENNY TALBOT, AGED 13

MILLENNIUM EXPERIENCE

IT IS THE YEAR 2999 and we are coming towards the end of the Millennium. It is the Christmas holidays. I am going to London to visit my father. He is an archaeologist. That means he digs up and studies old things. I am going on my own. It is my first trip away from home and I am really excited.

I look out of my glass bubble jet over the domes of London. In the old days people travelled in metal boxes called cars. Weird! From above, London looks like soapsuds, sitting in a sea of brown dust. Inside the domes I can see buildings and trees. Nothing lives outside anymore. It is too hot. I steer my bubble jet down towards the entry dome. As I land, I can see Dad waiting for me. He says he is working today but from tomorrow onwards he is free. I ask him if I can come with him and he says, "Yes".

When we get to the place where Dad works, I see enormous spikes sticking out of the ground in a circle. In the centre, half covered by dust and dirt, I can see the head and shoulders of a giant statue. All over the site people are digging and scraping away at the sand. Dad tells me that he is busy and will leave me with his friend Quazar. When we are alone, Quazar asks, "Would you like to hear the story of the Millennium Dome, Aurora?" Aurora is my name. We sit down next to a table laid out with hundreds of pieces of metal, all neatly labelled.

Quazar begins, "There are lots of stories about these spikes, but legend has it that a long, long time ago,

when people didn't live in bubbles and the world was covered in beautiful plants, animals and clear blue waters called seas, strange beings from Mars appeared on our Earth. It was a very dark night when nothing stirred. A blinding beam of light shone down from the heavens and Martians appeared. This was their landing site and they built their headquarters here. They didn't like humans, and if any humans came near, they would turn them to stone. Soon they had so many bodies they built a chamber around them in human shape and this is the remains of it."

Quazar stops to sip his ruby thoughtfully. (Ruby is a mixture of tea and artificial juice – tea is too precious to drink on its own). "Those signs," he continues, pointing at some large pieces of metal which say, very faintly, McDonalds and Wimpy, "were names of the most important Martians. Any humans that were captured were treated as their slaves. They had to cook, clean and carry stone bodies into the chamber. They had to make a cloth to put over the spikes to protect the Martians from the sun's powerful rays. It was a hard life. Soon the Martians couldn't cope with the heat on Earth and left. For centuries afterwards, the spikes were so hot nobody could touch them. Of course, all that was before the dust storms ..."

Just then, Dad comes back and takes me off for some ruby. I will never forget what Quazar told me, even if it isn't true. I know one thing is true though, Quazar is a very good storyteller! When we were saying goodbye, he gave me a tiny fragment of cloth. I put it in the pocket of my flying suit. I am going to take it home to show Mum in the New Year. Then it will be the Year 3000, the 31st century.

EMMA KATE DONNELLY, AGED 10

ACKNOWLEDGEMENTS

On behalf of FABLE (Forum for the Arts in Bromley for Learning in Education), we would like to thank the people and organisations listed below for their help in the production of this anthology.

Ken Davis, Director of Education and the Education Committee, who supported the project and let it happen

The children, young people, teachers and head teachers in Bromley schools for their creative energy

All the team at Standards and Effectiveness Services, but especially Pauline Lupton-Dewell, Gerry Rivett, Kevin Dyke and Sue Mordecai, for all their help and support

The team at Picthall & Gunzi Ltd, especially Chez Picthall,

Christiane Gunzi, Ray Bryant, Gillian Cooling, Anthony Cutting, Lauren Robertson, Floyd Sayers and Susan Stowers

Renate Keeping and the children of Bromley Road Infant School, Valley Primary School and The Ravensbourne School for their designs for the cover

The London Arts Board for Millennium Funding, and Ottakars Bookshop, National Westminster Bank and Bromley Central Library for their help in setting up the project

Pamela Smyth and Jay Mathews
Millennium Arts Project Directors

MILLENNIUM EVENTS

Throughout the year 2000 there will be a host of exhibitions, performances and other events taking place in schools, libraries and local venues around the country. In the London Borough of Bromley, schools are working together in small neighbourhood groups on a variety of *Millennium Arts Projects*, the first of which is this book. Other events involving Bromley Schools will include:

Fairfield Halls in February 2000

Dance and drama presentations, inspired by the stories and poems from '*Messages to the Future*', are taking place at the Fairfield Halls, Croydon, Surrey in February 2000. Led by dance and drama teachers, the groups of ten and 11 year olds are also putting on performances for their local neighbourhood groups. *Musical performances* of a new work called '*Millennium Tales*' will be performed at the Fairfield Halls by school choirs. This piece has been specially composed by Bob Chilcott.

Bromley Schools' Day in the Dome in May 2000

Children and young people from Bromley schools are invited to the Millennium Dome in Greenwich, London, in May 2000 as part of a national scheme sponsored by McDonalds. Extracts from the '*Millennium Tales*' music will be performed in the Dome during the day. A dance, drama and video work called '*Bromley Greats*' will be shown in the Dome to celebrate the lives of some of the famous people of Bromley, past and present. A selection of the work from Bromley schools' anthologies of poems, stories and pictures will be on display at the Dome.

Tapestries

Beautiful tapestries have been created by Bromley schools on the theme of the zones of the Millennium Dome. These colourful, highly textured pieces have been stitched and stuck, knitted and hooked by their parents and teachers. They will be on show at Bromley Library in December 1999 and January 2000. They will also be displayed at the Dome, thanks to the Millennium Tapestry Company.

Creativity in Bromley Schools

MILLENNIUM EXPERIENCE

Read on NATIONAL READING CAMPAIGN

fABLE

LONDON ARTS BOARD

Education Services

Bromley THE LONDON BOROUGH

A FINAL WORD...

Selecting the stories, poems and pictures for this book was an almost impossible task, as all the work deserved to be included. Wherever possible, we have tried to keep the children's 'voices' and have therefore not imposed strict rules of grammar or punctuation upon their work.